"What a fun book! First, Dotty Griffith begins with clear tut from scratch, along with lots of creative variations on the basic form. (I can't wait to try her cilantro lime corn tortillas.) She then shares a host of recipes for using your homemade bounty—everything from tacos to enchiladas and soups to desserts. Tips, history, and corny jokes are peppered throughout, also making for an enjoyable read. If you're a fan of all things tortilla, this cookbook is a must!"

—**Lisa Fain**, blogger at *Homesick Texan* and author of *The Homesick Texan Cookbook* and *Queso!*

"This book is the real deal for tortillas of all kinds as well as recipes using tortillas!"

—**Sylvia Casares**, chef/owner, Sylvia's Enchilada Kitchen, Houston, and author of *The Enchilada Queen Cookbook*

"Dotty Griffith has packed more about tortillas into one book that I thought possible. *The Ultimate Tortilla Press Cookbook* is the only reference you'll ever need to make all kinds of great tortillas."

—**John Mariani**, author of *The Dictionary of American Food and Drink* and *The Encyclopedia of American Food and Drink*

"Making tortillas at home is an easy, rewarding, and tasty craft to master. Dotty Griffith has written the definitive book on the subject, covering not just tortillas but all the amazing things you can make with them."

—**Cheryl Alters Jamison**, author of *Texas Slow Cooker* and co-author of *Smoke & Spice* and *Texas Home Cooking*

"With this book, Dotty Griffith ushers in a new age for the ancient tortilla."

—**Elaine Corn**, author of *Now You're Cooking* and *Now You're Cooking for Company*

"Dotty Griffith has written the book I've been waiting for all my life—and the one I wish I had written first! This brilliant book is destined to become a classic. This book will appeal to the curious but inexperienced cook with recipes like the rich and creamy, but simple Avocado Crema. It will also lure those wishing to be true tortilla aficionados, as Dotty takes you carefully through nixtamalization, the process for treating and grinding dried corn into fresh masa. From chimichangas to chilaquiles, from salsas to sopes, this book has everything you'll ever need to satisfy your cravings for all things tortilla."

—**Stephan Pyles**, chef, restaurateur, and author of *The New Texas Cuisine*

the *Ultimate*
TORTILLA PRESS
COOKBOOK

125 Recipes for all kinds of make-your-own tortillas—and for **burritos, enchiladas, tacos,** and more

DOTTY GRIFFITH

HARVARD COMMON PRESS

Inspiring | Educating | Creating | Entertaining

Brimming with creative inspiration, how-to projects, and useful information to enrich your everyday life, Quarto Knows is a favorite destination for those pursuing their interests and passions. Visit our site and dig deeper with our books into your area of interest: Quarto Creates, Quarto Cooks, Quarto Homes, Quarto Lives, Quarto Drives, Quarto Explores, Quarto Gifts, or Quarto Kids.

First Published in 2018 by The Harvard Common Press, an imprint of The Quarto Group, 100 Cummings Center, Suite 265-D, Beverly, MA 01915, USA.
T (978) 282-9590 F (978) 283-2742 QuartoKnows.com

The Harvard Common Press titles are also available at discount for retail, wholesale, promotional, and bulk purchase. For details, contact the Special Sales Manager by email at specialsales@quarto.com or by mail at The Quarto Group, Attn: Special Sales Manager, 401 Second Avenue North, Suite 310, Minneapolis, MN 55401, USA.

22 21 20 19 18   1 2 3 4 5

ISBN: 978-0-7603-5488-9

Library of Congress Cataloging-in-Publication Data

Names: Griffith, Dotty, author.
Title: The ultimate tortilla press cookbook : 125 recipes for all kinds of make-your-own tortillas and for burritos, enchiladas, quesadillas, tacos, and more that use them / Dotty Griffith.
Description: Beverly, MA, USA : Quarto Publishing Group USA, Inc., [2017]
Identifiers: LCCN 2017045649 | ISBN 9780760354889 (trade pbk.)
Subjects: LCSH: Mexican American cooking. | Tortillas. | LCGFT: Cookbooks.
Classification: LCC TX715.2.S69 G75 2017 | DDC 641.5926872073--dc23 LC record available at https://lccn.loc.gov/2017045649

Design and Page Layout: Laura Mcfadden Design Inc.
Photography: Kristin Teig

Printed in China

MIX
Paper from responsible sources
FSC® C104723

To Kelly, Caitlin, and Jack.
Press on.

CONTENTS

ABOUT TORTILLAS AND HOW TO MAKE THEM

part **1**

1

THE FLAT LINE OF HISTORY

Tortillas Then and Now

Pre-Columbian tortilla history goes back an estimated 10,000 years to Mesoamerica, where Mayans made tortillas from ground corn. The Aztecs continued the tradition, as did the Incas in South America.

The modern history of tortillas dates back to the 1519 Spanish invasions and conquest of the area Europeans considered New Spain, or, more widely, the New World. Today, we know this area as Mexico. The Aztecs thought of it as home.

What was novel to Hernando Cortez and his conquistadores was the equivalent of sliced bread to the native Aztecs. Indigenous people had been making round flatbreads of ground corn dough—what the Spanish named tortillas—for thousands of years. The Aztecs called their daily bread tlaxcalli (prononced *las-CAL-e*).

Today's tortillas aren't just made from corn, however. In 1519, Jews—many forced to convert or feign conversion to Catholicism—settled as far away from the Spanish capital as they could to avoid the Spanish inquisition as it played out in New Spain. They put down roots in what is now northern Mexico, from which flour tortillas emanated.

Jews who settled in what is today northern Mexico didn't consider corn as kosher; instead, they used wheat flour to make a flatbread-like tlaxcalli, as well as their staple matzo, or pita, depending on from where they immigrated. Flatbreads made from flour (i.e., flour tortillas) are the New World version of matzo.

Some Christian European transplants weren't big on peasant corn either. They considered wheat flour more akin to the body of Christ (i.e., communion wafers), so they, too, were fine with appropriating native corn flatbread techniques to make wheat flatbread.

HOLY TORTILLAS!

Regardless of the basic ingredients—corn masa or wheat flour—used for the flatbreads we know today simply as tortillas, both are made using similar techniques. Tortillas begin with a simple dough of ground corn, called *nixtamal*. From nixtamal, ancient tortilla makers pinched off golf ball-size pieces and flattened them by hand or by rolling with a rod or pin, before toasting on a hot, flat surface known today as a comal or griddle.

What isn't simple is the miracle of nixtamalization, the process for the preparation of maize that the Mesoamericans discovered. The chemical changes that occur during nixtamalization makes the difference between cornmeal (ground dried corn that can't form a dough) and *masa harina* (ground nixtamalized corn that can form a dough). Corn meal requires the addition of flour and liquid to form a dough. With masa harina, just add liquid.

BANNED IN LUBBOCK

Tossing tortillas onto the field is one of five deadly sins that can get a Texas Tech University student kicked out of a college football game at this Texas panhandle school of higher learning. Tech students have been throwing tortillas after kickoff at least since 1992. Some still do. In case you wondered, flour (not corn) tortillas are the edible Frisbees of choice. What else can get you booted?

1 Consuming alcohol.

2 Being too drunk. (Perhaps numbers 1 and 2 are a little redundant?)

3 Wearing the colors of another team.

4 Smoking (anything).

The chemical changes that occur make all the difference. To prepare nixtamal (the treated cornmeal), whole kernels of dried corn are soaked and cooked in a "slaked lime" or alkaline solution made with calcium hydroxide, called "cal" for short (see recipe page 42). Whole kernel nixtamal is also known as posole or hominy.

Fresh ground nixtamal is seldom used by modern home cooks because making it is a tedious and time-consuming process. Also, fresh nixtamal sours quickly. But if you live in an area where tortilla factories are accessible, you may be able to buy fresh nixtamal by the pound. Whether you make it or buy it, keep fresh nixtamal refrigerated and use within twenty-four hours.

On the other hand, masa harina—made from dried, ground nixtamal—is shelf stable and easily stored in bags. This is the form most commonly used by modern home cooks and is widely available in supermarkets, Hispanic groceries, and online through various sources.

Homemade Tortillas: Why Bother?

Most of us take tortillas for granted. They're relatively cheap to buy—and relatively good.

We use them just like the Mesoamericans who invented them: like bread. In fact, tortilla sales are second only to sliced bread in the United States.

So why make them? Why buy special equipment—such as electric or manual presses, rolling pins, griddles, or comals—to make from scratch what is so readily available in supermarkets, convenience stores, and specialty groceries? For the same reason we bake bread, biscuits, and rolls. Because just out of the oven or hot off the griddle, baked dough beckons, satisfies, and comforts like nothing else.

Fresh-made daily bread, including tortillas, is special because, for most of us, it is anything but a daily experience. Although making tortillas requires practice, making tortillas is faster and easier than making yeast bread, which requires mixing and kneading the dough, letting it rise once or twice, shaping, and baking it.

When it comes to homemade tortillas, the beauty is in the taste and the aroma. Don't sweat the symmetry. Get the tortillas as thin as possible but accept the fact that perfectly round tortillas with smooth edges are the products of machines. Practice will make your tortillas rounder and more uniform, especially flour tortillas. They probably won't ever be perfect, except in taste and authenticity.

As with fresh yeast bread or any quick bread, the aroma of fresh tortillas is enticing. Gently crispy on the outside and tender inside, fresh tortillas are a special treat. Even plain, but certainly with a pat of melting butter, cheese, or silky refried beans, homemade tortillas are a true gift from the special cook who knows how to make them.

Get your special on and become a tortilla talent.

There's yet another reason to make tortillas at home: control over ingredients. Your homemade tortillas will have no preservatives or other chemical additives for shelf stability, since your tortillas won't last long enough to need preservatives. Delicious as they are, your tortillas likely will be scarfed as soon as they come off the griddle.

Moreover, tortillas—originally made from corn—were gluten free before gluten free was cool. Corn doesn't contain gluten, although some of today's formulations for corn tortillas call for a bit of flour in the dough. This book has recipes for truly gluten-free tortillas (watch for recipes marked GF) made from corn masa (dough), as well as gluten free and alternate flours that produce tortillas good enough to stand in nicely for all-purpose or unbleached flour tortillas. If you want to be sure your masa harina is gluten free, only buy brands labeled "gluten free."

And then there's tortilla versatility. Tortillas wrap, stack, roll, and fold. They can be crispy or soft, plain or flavored. They partner naturally with almost any flavor profile, protein, and vegetables in almost every form. There's no limit to how they can be consumed.

Still, we had to start and stop somewhere. Most of the recipes in this book represent dishes beloved in the southwestern United States, America's Tortilla Belt. The states of Texas, New Mexico, Arizona, and California link the conchos of this culinary girdle.

Come on! It's time for a fresh take on tortillas.

TOP DOG

Tortillas have outsold hamburger and hot dog buns at supermarkets and retail food stores since 2010.

2 MEET THE PRESS

Start with the Right Equipment

When it comes to creating successful tortillas, preparation is 90 percent of the inspiration. Getting the right gear is the first step to make great tortillas—corn and flour.

Start with the press. First, decide whether you want to go manual or electric. If you opt for manual, you will then need to decide what sort of griddle or comal you will use to bake your tortillas. No matter whether you go manual or electric, you will need a few other tools, such as rolling pins, griddles, and warmers. Also, you'll need plastic bags for storage, if you have any leftover tortillas—which isn't likely.

PRESS ADVISORY

Here are some tortilla press recommendations based on my experience:

- For fresh corn tortillas, stay low tech. Use a hand-operated heavy cast-iron press, such as the kind made by Victoria. Cook the tortillas on a heavy cast-iron griddle or comal. Corn tortillas tend to break apart in an electric press.

- For fresh flour tortillas, an electric press and toaster make pressing to the proper thickness much easier. I had the greatest success with CucinaPro. One caveat: The bottom toasting plate doesn't get hot enough to make the tortillas bubble or to produce dark char marks. The flavor difference is discernable, especially with tortillas made from fresh lard. If you like darker char marks, press flour tortillas in the electric press, parcook, and finish them on a traditional griddle or comal.

MANUAL OR ELECTRIC?

Consider the advantages of going with a manual press. The biggest investment you'll need to make is in a quality, heavy metal press. Cast iron is recommended. The handle on cheap aluminum and plastic models will bend and break under the pressure required to flatten the tortillas. You'll also need a flat pan on which to cook tortillas. If you already have a griddle or crepe pan (stove top or electric), you do not need to buy a designated tortilla pan (unless you choose to do so).

If you want to opt out of having to use elbow grease, however, consider an electric tortilla maker. In general, the electric press costs twice as much or more than a manual press. This two-function machine flattens the tortilla dough and toasts the tortillas between the same plates. It looks like a flat surface waffle iron.

SWEAT THE DETAILS

Here are some factors to consider when deciding what equipment to buy:

Cost: A heavy duty cast-iron press costs about half or less than half the cost of an electric tortilla press/toaster. (A rolling pin for flour tortillas is truly cheapo.) Also, it is likely that you already have other equipment used to make tortillas, like a griddle, so you won't have to make another major investment.

Storage: A manual press requires about the same amount of space as an electric machine. Either can be stored upright to take up less space.

Convenience: An electric tortilla machine can make the process of rolling or pressing easier and faster, and it doesn't require a second appliance or pan for toasting because an electric press/toaster allows you to press and then toast in the same appliance. A manual press requires you to press or roll the tortillas and then toast on a flat-bottom appliance or pan, such as a pancake griddle, crepe pan, or comal.

Even though the electric process is one step, it requires some practice to learn how to use any press, whether manual or electric. But once you learn how to operate an electric press, you can turn out a dozen or more tortillas pretty quickly. Also, most electric press/toasters can also be used for roti and chapatti (forms of Indian bread), pita, focaccia, gyro, and moo shu pancakes.

Degree of difficulty: While Mesoamericans patted out corn tortillas with their hands or rolled them, most tortilla bakers today use a manual press to flatten balls of dough into thin rounds. Still, it takes practice, and some strength, to get the tortillas thin enough, as well as to learn how to cook them. Occasionally, you may want to use a rolling pin to flatten them some more once the press has done its best.

Flour tortillas, on the other hand, can be rolled by hand using a rolling pin. Most indigenous flour tortilla bakers do it this way. The technique is passed from generation to generation. For beginning tortilla makers—especially those who didn't grow up making them—rolling flour tortillas requires practice to get the tortillas thin enough and to achieve consistency in size and shape.

Though somewhat automated, electric tortilla makers have their own learning curve. First, you must perfect the corn masa or flour dough. Then, you must master the machine that flattens and then toasts the tortillas. There's simply no magic wand for fresh, homemade tortillas, although there is a machine (colloquially known as the Keurig for tortillas) in development. Insert a pod and out comes a tortilla!

In the meantime, for sublime tortillas learn to make them yourself. But don't expect perfection, except in taste and texture. You can achieve that in relatively short order. And no matter whether you are making corn or flour tortillas using your hands, a press, or a rolling pin, don't be disappointed if they're not perfectly round. Only commercial, machine-made tortillas are perfectly round with smooth edges. You're not a machine! Making them thin enough also takes practice. Concentrate on thin and delicious more than on symmetry.

DOTTY'S PICKS FOR TOP-RATED TORTILLA PRESSES

MANUAL

Victoria Cast Iron Tortilla Press and Pataconera
- Eight-inch (20 cm) diameter
- Original made in Colombia
- Under $30

IMUSA Cast Iron Tortilla Press
- Eight-inch (20 cm) diameter
- Under $30

ELECTRIC

Saachi SA1650 Electric Non-Stick Roti Chapati Flat Bread Wraps/Tortilla Maker with Temperature Control
- Under $50

CucinaPro 1443 Flatbread and Tortilla Maker
- Under $70

Chef Pro 10-Inch Tortilla Maker/Flat Bread Maker
- Under $100

DOTTY'S BOTTOM LINE

After using multiple brands of electric and manual presses, here are my recommendations on what to use:

For corn tortillas: A heavy manual press, such as the Victoria Cast Iron Tortilla Press, produces the thinnest tortillas. Cooking the tortillas on a well-seasoned cast-iron griddle or comal result in the best consistency—pliable but with a light crust on the outside with the essence of soft masa inside.

The downside of using an electric press is that corn tortillas don't get the beautiful char spots that can be obtained with a comal. Also, if pressed too hard, the press can release a burst of steam and tear the tortillas.

For flour tortillas: CucinaPro produces the flattest, most evenly cooked flour tortillas of all the electric machines I tried. The downside of using this press is that the cooking plate doesn't get hot enough to produce beautiful char spots. Still, this is the easiest machine to press and cook on. The result is a thin, evenly toasted flour tortilla. Be sure to remove the tortillas before they cook through, though, or they won't be pliable enough to roll.

It is easy to learn to roll flour tortillas by hand. Though they tend to be a bit thicker, tortillas rolled by hand and cooked on a comal are as satisfying and beckoning as homemade biscuits. The aroma of wheat dough browning is incomparable.

3
A TORTILLA TUTORIAL

The secret to great homemade tortillas, whether you are making them from corn, another gluten-free base, or wheat flour, is to get them thin enough. That's where the press comes in.

Let's first go through the process for corn tortillas using a manual and then an electric press. Then, we'll discuss how to finish them by toasting them on a griddle or on an all-in-one electric press and griddle. Finally, we'll do the same for flour and gluten-free tortillas.

Corn Tortilla Know-How

PRESSING AND BAKING CORN TORTILLAS

Prepare the masa for corn tortillas (page 38). Divide the masa into orbs the size of golf balls for 6-inch (15 cm) tortillas or thereabout. Smaller balls of masa produce smaller corn tortillas about four inches (10 cm) in diameter (for street tacos, for example). Six inches (15 cm) is about the maximum diameter for making corn tortillas. Press each ball of masa to form tortillas. Cook each immediately (page 29).

Using a Manual Tortilla Press

Cut two pieces (square or round) of durable plastic from a food storage bag or clean shopping bag. Pieces should be one inch (2.5 cm) larger than the diameter of the tortilla press. Parchment paper also works. You will use these pieces of plastic or parchment paper to line the surfaces of the top and bottom plates of the press. For good measure, make two or three pairs in case the first pair tears or gets sticky.

When ready to press a corn tortilla:

1   Line the bottom press with a piece of plastic or parchment paper.

2   Wet your hands to prevent sticking. Use your fingers and palms to somewhat flatten one ball of masa at a time into a thick disc, 2 to 3 inches (5 to 7.5 cm) in diameter.

3   Place the disc of masa in the center of the lined bottom press. Center the second piece of plastic or parchment paper over the masa. Firmly press down the top plate. Wiggle the press handle slightly from side to side to evenly distribute the masa. Lift the top plate. Rotate the tortilla 180 degrees (a half turn) and firmly press again to make a 6-inch (15 cm) tortilla as thin as possible.

4   If a slightly thinner tortilla is desired, remove the tortilla from the press by lifting the edges of the plastic. Use a rolling pin to press the plastic-covered tortilla a little thinner.

5   When the tortilla is at the desired thickness, lift off the top piece of plastic. Flip the tortilla into your other hand and peel off the top layer of plastic. Use a spatula or your fingers to flip the tortilla onto a preheated comal or griddle (page 29). Reuse the pieces of plastic until they tear or become sticky.

Note: These steps are not intended to replace the manufacturer's directions. Please refer to the owner's manual.

Using an Electric Tortilla Press

Electric presses flatten the tortillas between two plates and toast them on the bottom plate. The presses look like waffle machines with smooth plates (instead of patterned plates). These combination press/cookers have two handles. One is known as the "shaping" mechanism—the first step for making flour tortillas. The other is a lever for "pressing" a tortilla. This mechanism is applied to corn and flour tortillas to flatten them before cooking. You cook the tortillas on the bottom plate and must flip the tortilla to cook both sides. Do not cook in a closed press.

STEP BY STEP

When using a manual press for corn tortillas, follow the steps in this order:

1   Make masa and form golf ball–size rounds (page 38). Keep moist (page 38).

2   Preheat the comal (page 29).

3   Press a tortilla (page 26).

4   Cook the tortilla on a hot, flat surface (page 29).

5   Keep warm in a tortilla warmer. This step allows the tortilla to steam and soften for pliability (page 33).

6   Repeat until all the dough is used.

When ready to press a corn tortilla:

1 Preheat the machine per the user manual instructions.

2 Wet your hands to prevent sticking. Use your fingers and palms to somewhat flatten one ball of masa at a time into a thick disc, 2 to 3 inches (5 to 7.5 cm) in diameter.

3 Using a paper towel, lightly wipe each plate with vegetable oil.

4 Place the slightly flattened piece of dough closer to the handle of the bottom plate. Close the lid and push down on the pressing handle to flatten the dough. The thickness should be no more than ⅛ inch (3 mm), or a little less than a hardbound book cover. Next, lift the lid slightly to release the steam. Close the lid and cook for 10 seconds longer.

5 Open the press and using a spatula, flip the tortilla. Cook for 10 more seconds or until brown spots appear on both sides. Transfer to a tortilla warmer. Proceed with the remaining dough.

6 Hold tortillas in a warmer to keep them warm, soft, and supple (page 33).

Note: These steps are not intended to replace the manufacturer's directions. Please refer to the owner's manual.

When cooking corn tortillas on a comal:

1 Preheat a comal or griddle over medium-high heat to about 375°F (190°C). The surface is ready when water sprinkled on the hot surface bubbles or "dances" and immediately evaporates.

2 Before cooking the corn tortillas, use a wad of paper towel to spread a light layer of vegetable oil on the surface of the preheated comal. Or lightly spray with vegetable oil.

3 Cook the corn tortilla for about 15 seconds on the preheated cooking surface. This step sets the dough. Flip the corn tortilla and cook for about 1 minute. Flip the tortilla again and cook for about 1 minute longer on the first side. Cool slightly and then transfer to a tortilla warmer to keep the corn tortillas warm, soft, and supple (page 33).

STEP BY STEP

When using an electric press for corn tortillas, follow the steps in this order:

1 Make the masa and form golf ball-size rounds (page 38). Keep moist (page 33).

2 Preheat the machine (page 29).

3 Press a tortilla (page 29).

4 Cook the tortilla (page 29).

5 Keep warm in a tortilla warmer. This steps allows the tortilla to steam and soften for pliability (page 33).

6 Repeat until all the dough is used.

Flour Tortilla Know-How

Now, let's work our way through the steps for flour tortillas using both a manual and an electric press. We'll also discuss how to finish them by toasting on a griddle or an all-in-one electric press and griddle.

SHAPING AND BAKING FLOUR TORTILLAS

Here's a quick step by step for shaping and baking flour tortillas:

1   Prepare the dough for Basic Flour Tortillas (page 50).

2   Return the dough to the mixing bowl or place in a clean bowl. Lay a piece of plastic wrap directly on the dough. Cover that with a cloth kitchen towel. Let rest for 30 to 60 minutes or up to 6 hours.

3   After allowing the dough to rest, knead lightly. Divide the dough into orbs the size of golf balls for 6-inch (15 cm) tortillas. Slightly larger balls, like clementines, can be pressed into 10-inch (25 cm) tortillas for burritos and wraps. The thickness should be no more than ⅛ inch (3 mm), or a little less than a hardbound book cover. Cover with plastic and a towel until you're ready to roll out the tortillas.

To Roll Flour Tortillas by Hand and Bake

1   Lightly coat a pastry board with flour. Using a rolling pin, press from the center to the edge. Flip the dough and rotate 180 degrees each time you press with the rolling pin. To prevent sticking, lightly sprinkle the surface of the tortilla with a small amount of flour each time you flip and turn the dough. The thickness should be no more than ⅛ inch (3 mm) or a little less than a hardbound book cover. Stack the tortillas between pieces of waxed paper and keep covered until all tortillas are rolled.

2   Preheat the comal to 400ºF (200ºC). When the comal is hot, lightly coat the surface with vegetable oil using a wad of paper towel or lightly coat with cooking oil spray.

STEP BY STEP

When rolling flour tortillas by hand:

1   Make the dough and let rest (page 50). Form golf ball-size rounds (page 31). Keep moist (page 52).

2   Preheat the comal (page 31).

3   Roll the tortillas and keep moist (page 31) until all are flattened into tortillas and ready to bake.

4   Cook the tortillas on a hot, flat surface (page 31) one or two at a time until are all baked.

5   Keep them warm in a tortilla warmer. This steps allows the tortillas to steam and soften for pliability (page 33).

A small hand roller like this can be helpful to achieve that last little bit of thinness and round the edges of the tortilla.

3   Place a tortilla on the comal. Using a spatula, flip the tortilla when a few bubbles break the surface, after about 30 seconds. Cook the other side, another 30 seconds or until the tortilla has a few light brown spots on each side.

4   Repeat with the remaining tortillas, oiling the surface of the comal as needed.

5   Cool slightly and then transfer to a tortilla warmer to keep the tortillas warm, soft, and supple (page 33).

To Flatten and Bake Flour Tortillas Using an Electric Press/Toaster

1 Preheat the machine.

2 Use your fingers and palms to somewhat flatten one ball of dough at a time into a thick disc, about 2 to 3 inches (5 to 7.5 cm) in diameter.

3 Place the slightly flattened piece of dough just a bit closer to the handle of the bottom plate. Close the lid and gently press down on the shaping handles to flatten the dough. If the dough slides forward, use a spatula to keep the dough in place as you gently press down.

4 Lift the lid slightly to release the steam. Gently press and release several times. Each press should be less than a second. If you press and hold, the steam won't escape and will cause the flour tortilla to split and break.

5 Raise the lid and rotate the partially flattened dough about 180 degrees.

6 Press and release again several more times, further flattening the ball of dough.

7 Raise the lid and rotate the dough another 180 degrees.

8 Now is the time to apply the pressure. Use the pressing handle to press the flour tortilla to the final thinness. Firmly press and release several times to achieve desired thinness, no more than ⅛ inch (3 mm), or a little less than a hardbound book cover.

9 Brown the tortilla until there are dark brown spots on both sides. You should bake in the open position. When one side is brown, use a spatula to flip the tortilla and brown the other side.

10 Cool slightly and then transfer to a tortilla warmer to keep tortillas warm, soft, and supple (page 33).

11 Repeat until all the dough is used.

Note: These steps are not intended to replace manufacturer's directions. Please refer to the owner's manual.

Manual and Electric Tortilla Rollers

There are also manual and electric tortilla rollers that look like pasta machines.

1 Wet your hands to prevent sticking. Use your fingers and palms to somewhat flatten one ball of masa at a time into a thick disc, about 2 to 3 inches (5 to 7.5 cm) in diameter.

2 Place the edge of a disc of masa at the top of the rollers. Wind the rollers or turn on the machine to force the masa through the rollers and push out a tortilla. Thickness should be no more than ⅛ inch (3 mm), or a little less than a hardbound book cover. You will need to cook it on a comal or griddle (page 31).

STEP BY STEP

When shaping and baking flour tortillas using an electric press:

1 Make the dough and let rest (page 50). Form golf ball-size rounds. Keep moist (page 52).

2 Preheat the machine (page 32).

3 Use the shaping handles to flatten balls of dough.

4 Use the pressing lever to achieve the desired thinness of flour tortilla.

5 Cook the flour tortillas on the bottom plate (page 32).

6 Keep warm in a tortilla warmer. This steps allows the tortilla to steam and soften for pliability (page 33).

7 Repeat until all the dough is used.

Keeping Homemade Tortillas Warm

Whether you are making flour or corn tortillas, you want to keep them warm off the griddle for serving. This step is very important to produce pliable tortillas. For this, you need a tortilla warmer. There are several variations of them. Some are round, ovenproof stoneware or thick plastic containers with lids. Many are microwave-safe. Others are made of cloth with insulated lining. Wrapping a stack of hot tortillas with clean towels and/or foil can also do the job. This steams them for pliability and keeps them hot. Serve warm as soon after toasting as possible.

Storing and Using Day-Old Homemade Tortillas

Most of the time, you will consume all the tortillas you can make in one sitting and still want more. Fresh, homemade corn tortillas simply don't store well beyond a day. However, if you do want to save some, place them in a plastic storage bag while still a little warm but not hot. This will trap the moisture. Press out the air and seal. Refrigerate no more than one day for best results.

Freezing homemade corn tortillas tends to dry out and crack them. Still, don't throw them away. On the outside chance you actually made more fresh corn tortillas than you could consume and froze (rather than discarded) them, consider some of the classic uses for stale and broken corn tortillas. See recipes such as Tortilla Soup (page 170), Migas (page 147), and Chilaquiles (page 146).

Fresh, homemade flour tortillas store with more success. Place them in a plastic storage bag at room temperature. Press out any excess air. Store for no more than one day. Freeze them after that if you must. Again, don't worry about waste. If, and that's a big IF, you have uneaten fresh flour tortillas, please see recipes such as Flour Tortilla "Fried Dumplings" (page 186), Flour Tortilla "Empanadas" (page 192), and Quesadillas (page 119).

EXPERT ADVICE FROM SYLVIA CASARES,
author of *The Enchilada Queen Cookbook*

"Please, do not ruin your precious, handmade flour tortillas by reheating in a microwave. The result is a rubbery texture. You'll be sorry you went to the trouble to make them if you zap to reheat."

Sylvia's a purist. You've been warned. To reheat flour tortillas, wrap them in foil and reheat in the oven at 300°F (150°C, or gas mark 2), or heat through on both sides on a hot comal or griddle. Or try the other methods on page 34.

HOW TO KEEP LOTS OF TORTILLAS HOT

Need to keep a large amount of tortillas hot? Like for a party or big family dinner? Place hot tortillas in an ice (insulated) chest lined with a towel.

REHEATING TORTILLAS

Ways to reheat fresh-made or store-bought tortillas:

Dry heat: This method is used for tortillas made that day. Heat on a griddle or skillet. Flip until pliable.

Hot vegetable oil: Use hot vegetable oil to soften and heat corn tortillas for enchiladas and tacos. Fry until soft or until golden brown for crispy.

Oven: Preheat the oven to 300°F (150ºC, or gas mark 2). Stack tortillas and wrap tightly in foil. Place in the oven for 20 minutes.

Steam: This is an excellent method for warming tortillas by the dozens. Pour one-half inch (1 cm) of water in the bottom of a steamer. Line the steamer basket with a thick, clean kitchen towel. Lay the tortillas in the basket in stacks of twelve. Small steamers hold one stack. Larger Asian steamers can hold several. Fold the edges of the towel over the tortillas to cover. Cover the steamer with the lid. Bring the water to a boil for 60 seconds and then turn off heat. Let stand for 15 minutes. Do not remove the lid. To keep warmer longer, place the steamer into a warming oven or reheat the water occasionally.

Microwave: If you wish to defy the Enchilada Queen (see sidebar, page 33), note that this method works best for no more than a dozen tortillas. Sprinkle a clean kitchen towel or several paper towels with 2 to 3 tablespoons (30 to 45 ml) of water. Wring or fold towels to distribute moisture. Line an 8- or 9-inch (20 or 23 cm) microwave-safe bowl, tortilla warmer, or casserole dish with the moistened towel(s). Add the stack of tortillas. Fold the towel over the tortillas. Cover the casserole or warmer with the lid or improvise with a microwave-safe dinner plate. Heat on 50 percent power for 4 minutes. Let stand 2 to 3 minutes. Tortillas will stay warm for up to 20 minutes.

EXPERT ADVICE FROM LESLEY TELLEZ,
author of *Mexican Street Food*

Plastic shopping bags make the best lining for the plates of a manual tortilla press. Trim single layer pieces of clean shopping bags so they are large enough to hang an inch (2.5 cm) over the edges of the plates on the press.

4.

LET'S MAKE SOME TORTILLAS

You've got the right stuff, so let's make some tortillas. This chapter includes recipes for corn and flour tortillas, as well as tortillas made from gluten-free wheat flour and alternative, non-wheat flours. A GF icon above the recipe name indicates the recipe is gluten free.

CORN TORTILLAS

Makes 12 tortillas

| 2 cups (240 g) masa harina, white or yellow | 2 to 3 tablespoons (16 to 24 g) all-purpose, unbleached, or (18 to 27 g) gluten-free flour (optional) | ½ teaspoon salt | 1¼ to 1⅓ cups (285 to 315 ml) warm water (more as needed) or Flavor-Infused Liquid (page 39) |

Maseca brand masa harina dominates the market. But there are others, too, so branch out if you like. The addition of a little flour can make corn tortilla dough easier to handle. *Do not add regular flour if you want gluten-free corn tortillas.*

1   In a medium bowl, whisk or stir together the masa and flour, if using, and salt.

2   Gradually add the water and mix, using a wooden spoon or spatula and hands, until the ingredients are well-blended. Knead for 20 to 30 seconds until the dough is pliable. The dough should be moist enough to hold together. Add additional warm water, 1 tablespoon (15 ml) at a time, if needed.

3   Divide the dough into 12 golf ball–size orbs, shaping with your hands. Place each dough ball in a bowl and cover with a damp towel to keep moist.

4   Press or roll each dough ball using a manual tortilla press or rolling pin and cook on 2 hot comal or griddle (page 29). Or press and toast using an electric tortilla press/toaster (page 26).

5   Keep warm (page 33) until all the dough is used.

Q: *Have you heard the joke about the tortilla?*

Don't bother. It's corny.

About Flavored Corn Tortillas

Flavoring and coloring corn tortillas is simply a matter of adding things to the basic dough. This can be done two ways: by adding dried herbs and spices or by infusing the tortillas with a flavored liquid.

Use them in any recipe for corn tortillas. Suggested uses are included.

HOW TO SPICE HOMEMADE CORN TORTILLAS

Use ground spices, such as red chile or chili powder, pureed black beans (page 173) in the dry ingredients.

For Cumin Corn Tortillas: Add 1 tablespoon (7 g) of ground dried cumin to 2 cups (240 g) of masa harina and use as directed for Corn Tortillas (page 38).

Suggested uses: Fried Tortilla Chips (page 110), Loaded Nachos (page 112), Mexican Street Tacos (page 130).

For Garlic Corn Tortillas: Add 1 tablespoon (10 g) of granulated garlic or 2 teaspoons of garlic powder (or to taste) to 2 cups (240 g) masa harina and use as directed for Corn Tortillas (page 38).

Suggested uses: Fried Tortilla Chips (page 110), Puffy Tacos (page 126), with Pinto or Black Bean Soup (page 173).

For Chile con Corn Tortillas: Add ⅛ to ¼ cup (15 to 30 g) (depending on desired heat level) of ground dried red chile or chili powder to 2 cups (240 g) of masa harina and use as directed for Corn Tortillas (page 38).

Suggested uses: Fried Tortilla Chips (page 110), Stacked Chicken Enchiladas (page 156) with Spicy Chicken (page 74).

For Black Bean Corn Tortillas: Drain 1 cup (240 g) of canned black beans. In work bowl of food processor, combine the drained black beans with 2 cups (240 g) masa harina (flour, if using) and salt. Process until all the ingredients are well-blended. Proceed as directed for Corn Tortillas (page 38).

Suggested uses: Baja Fish Tacos (page 132), Veggie Enchiladas (page 161), Breakfast Tacos (page 134) with Mexican-Style Breakfast Potatoes (page 139).

HOW TO FLAVOR-INFUSE CORN TORTILLAS

Once you get "the feel" of good masa, adjusting the proportions somewhat to get the right consistency of the dough will come naturally to you, and your flavored tortillas will be foolproof.

For Cilantro and Cumin Corn Tortillas: In a blender jar, combine 1 cup (16 g) of loosely packed cilantro leaves, 1 tablespoon (7 g) of ground cumin (or 2 tablespoons (12 g) of whole cumin seeds), and 1¼ cups (285 ml) of water. Process until smooth, about 1 minute. Use as directed for Corn Tortillas (page 38).

Suggested uses: Fried Tortilla Chips (page 110), Beef Enchiladas with Tex-Mex Chili Gravy (page 90), Taco Salad (page 165).

For Cilantro Lime Corn Tortillas: In a blender jar, combine 1 cup (16 g) of loosely packed cilantro leaves, 1 tablespoon (15 ml) of lime juice, and 1¼ cups (285 ml) of water. Process until smooth, about 1 minute. Use as directed for Corn Tortillas (page 38).

Suggested uses: Fried Tortilla Chips (page 110) with Guacamole (page 105), Baja Fish Tacos (page 132), Stacked Shrimp or Crab Enchiladas (page 157) with Tomato and Green Chile Sauce (page 92).

WEED FEED

As marijuana products become legal, watch for marijuana-infused *masa* for tortillas, gorditas, and sopes. Hot off the comal, they're delicious with Canna Butter, i.e. cannabis laced.

For Red Chile Corn Tortillas: Remove the stems and seeds from enough dried red chiles (such as pasilla, ancho, or guajillo) to make 1 cup (37 g), lightly packed. Rinse the chillies with cool water. Place the chillies and 1¼ cups (285 ml) of water in a medium saucepan over high heat. Bring to a boil and then reduce the heat and simmer for 15 minutes. Set aside off the heat for 10 minutes. In a blender jar or work bowl of a food processor, process the chillies and their liquid until smooth, about 1 minute. Pour the pureed chilli mixture through a fine strainer into a small bowl, pressing with the back of a spoon to extract as much liquid as possible; discard the solids. Add enough water to make 1¼ to 1⅓ cups (285 to 315 ml) of liquid. Use as directed for Corn Tortillas (page 38).

Suggested uses: Cheese Enchiladas (page 158) with Queso (page 99), Arizona Cheese Crisps (page 114), Migas (page 147).

For Roasted Green Chile Corn Tortillas: Roast 2 large poblanos, 4 to 5 jalapeños, 6 to 8 serranos, or other desired fresh chillies (page 40) to make ½ cup (72 g) peeled, seeded, and finely chopped roasted chiles. Place the chopped chillies and 1¼ cups (285 ml) of water in a blender container or the work bowl of a food processor. Process until smooth, about 1 minute. Use as directed for Corn Tortillas (page 38).

Suggested uses: Roast or Hot Smoked Duck (page 75), Mexican Street Tacos (page 130) with Pork (page 71) and Refried Black Beans (page 83), Nacho's Nachos (page 111).

For Toasted Garlic Corn Tortillas: Peel enough garlic cloves to make 1 cup (136 g). Place the cloves in single layer in a heavy skillet over medium-high heat. Toast until golden on one side, about 3 to 4 minutes. Turn and toast until golden on all sides, about 3 to 4 minutes longer. Remove from the pan and allow to cool. Place the toasted garlic cloves and 1¼ cups (285 ml) of water in a blender container or the work bowl of a food processor. Process until smooth, about 1 minute. Use as directed for Corn Tortillas (page 38).

Suggested uses: Loaded Nachos (page 112), Veggie Enchiladas (page 161) and New Mexico Red Chile Sauce (page 91), Breakfast Tacos (page 134) with Scrambled Eggs (page 136).

ROASTING FRESH CHILES

To roast fresh chiles (such as poblanos, jalapeños, bell peppers, or any other chile): Rinse and dry the peppers. Place in a heavy skillet over high heat or in a heavy sheet pan under a high heat broiler. When the skin on the heat side blackens and blisters, turn and roast some more until all the sides are blistered and blackened. Cover the skillet with a lid or place the roasted peppers in a heavy plastic bag with zipper. Press out all the air, seal, and allow to cool enough to handle, about 10 minutes. Using your fingers and the tip of a sharp paring knife, slip the skin off the roasted peppers. Rinse the peppers to remove the seeds. Discard any stems. Use as directed in recipes.

HOMEMADE NIXTAMAL

Makes 2 pounds (910 g) nixtamal or masa, about 16 tortillas

2 cups (448 g) dried dent corn (see sidebar, page 43), rinsed and drained

2 tablespoons (12 g) calcium hydroxide, aka "cal" (slaked or pickling lime)

6 cups (1.4 L) lukewarm water

1 teaspoon salt

If you want to try corn tortillas made from fresh nixtamal, you've got two options: Buy nixtamal (ground dried corn with "cal") at a Mexican grocery or from a tortilla factory or make it yourself. Please note that fresh nixtamal sours quickly, so use it right away. Store it tightly covered in the coolest part of refrigerator (or place in waterproof packaging and place in a bowl of ice and set inside the refrigerator, like you would fresh fish) no longer than overnight.

To make nixtamal, you need calcium hydroxide, called "cal" for short, and also known as pickling lime, and dried dent corn, usually found in Mexican markets and Latin groceries, as well as from various online sources.

Making nixtamal into masa also requires some kind of corn grinder to mill the soaked corn. The most basic and traditional manual implement is the classic Mexican or South American metate, a mealing stone of volcanic rock that looks like a tabletop anvil. Instead of a hammer, a stone rolling pin (known as a *mano*) is used to crush the grain against the surface of the metate.

Electric and manual (hand-cranked) corn mills are also an option. So is a large (not a mini) food processor. Since that's something most of us who are ambitious enough to make nixtamal will have, the recipe includes directions for grinding nixtamal using a food processor.

1   In a large saucepan over low heat, combine the corn, cal, and water. Bring to a boil, about 30 to 45 minutes. The water must heat slowly. As soon as the water boils, turn off the heat and let sit overnight, 18 to 24 hours, at room temperature.

2   Drain the soaked corn in a large colander. Rinse well with cold water.

3   Fill a deep bowl or large pan with cold water. Add the soaked corn. Use your hands to rub the corn in the water and remove the hulls. Pour off the water to remove any floating hulls. Refill with water to cover the corn, rub the corn, and pour off the water. Repeat 7 to 10 times to dehull the corn. When the water runs clear or near clear, mission accomplished. Do not drain the last time. At this point, you have posole. Posole is used in Mexican stews (page 175).

Q: *Did you hear the one about the tortilla?*
It fell flat.

NEED TO KNOW

Dent corn is a type of grain corn used to make tortillas. It is starchier and less sweet than sweet corn, the kind humans eat on and off the cob. Dent corn gets its name because there is a depression or dent in the top of the kernels.

4 For masa: Grind the dehulled corn to a smooth, fine textured dough (nixtamal) using a manual or electric grinder, metate, or food processor.

5 To make *masa* using a food processor, use a slotted spoon to drain half the excess liquid and place half of the soaked corn into the work bowl outfitted with blade. Pulse 10 to 15 times. Add the remaining corn and pulse 10 to 15 times. Add 1 to 2 tablespoons (15 to 28 ml) of water from the corn. Pulse another 8 to 10 times. Scrape the bowl as needed in between pulsing. Add 1 to 2 more tablespoons (15 to 28 ml) of water and salt. Pulse until a dough begins to form.

6 Turn out onto a board, knead a couple of times, and shape into a ball. Wrap with plastic and let set for 30 minutes. Break into 1½-ounce (42 g) pieces and shape into 16 balls.

7 Press each dough ball using a tortilla press (page 26).

8 Cook on a hot comal or griddle (page 29).

9 Or press and toast using an electric tortilla press/toaster (page 26).

10 Keep warm (page 33) until all the dough is used.

BLUE CORN TORTILLAS

Makes 12 tortillas

2 cups (240 g) blue corn masa harina

2 to 3 tablespoons (16 to 24 g) all-purpose, unbleached, or (18 to 27 g) gluten-free flour (optional)

½ teaspoon salt

1¼ to 1⅓ cups (285 to 315 ml) warm water (more as needed)

Blue corn is a central Mexico thing that has become a signature of Native American cooking, particularly in Arizona and New Mexico. Hopi and Navajo cultures rely on blue corn.

Tortillas can be made from blue corn masa harina pretty much the same way yellow and white corn tortillas are made. Minsa and Maseca are two prominent brands. Blue corn tortillas can also be made using blue cornmeal with the addition of flour.

Besides a lovely color that can range from blue to purple, blue corn has a light, nutty flavor. Some advocates promote blue corn as more nutritious than other forms of corn. Like all tortillas, those made from blue corn can also be fried for chips or used in other dishes that call for tortillas.

These may be used with any recipe calling for corn tortillas but are especially good with dishes using chicken and pork. *Do not add regular flour if you want gluten-free blue corn tortillas.*

1   In a medium bowl, whisk or stir together the masa and flour, if using, and salt.

2   Add the water. Mix, using a wooden spoon or spatula and hands, until all the ingredients are well-blended. Knead for 20 to 30 seconds until the dough is pliable. The dough should be moist enough to hold together. Add warm water, 1 tablespoon (15 ml) at a time, if needed.

3   Divide the dough into 12 golf ball–size orbs, shaping with your hands. Place each dough ball in a bowl and cover with a damp towel to keep moist.

4   Press or roll each dough ball using a manual tortilla press (page 26) or rolling pin and cook on a hot comal or griddle (page 29). Or press and toast using an electric tortilla press/toaster (page 26).

5   Keep warm (page 33) until all the dough is used.

12 IF BY HAND, 21,000 IF BY MACHINE

Five workers using modern machinery can pump out 21,000 tortillas an hour.

FRIED CORNMEAL PATTIES

Makes 4 servings

2 cups (240 g) yellow, white, or blue cornmeal

1 teaspoon salt

1 cup (235 ml) boiling water

Oil for frying

If this book was about Southern cooking, this recipe would be corn pone. If the focus was early American regional cuisine, they'd be johnnycakes. No matter what you call these fried cornmeal patties, they are a simple substitute for sopes. They're easier to make because these can be prepared in one step. Deep-fried, these cornmeal discs can be topped with the same ingredients that fill sopes and gorditas.

1 In a large mixing bowl, combine the cornmeal and salt. Gradually stir in the boiling water. The dough should be moist enough to hold a shape but not too soft. Allow the dough to cool enough to handle, about 5 minutes.

2 Divide the dough into 12 golf ball–size orbs, shaping it with your hands.

3 Using your hands, flatten each ball of dough into ½-inch (13 mm) thick patty. While the oil heats, cover the patties with a damp towel.

4 Heat ½-inch (13 mm) of oil in an electric skillet to 375°F (190°C), or use a heavy skillet over medium-high heat and a candy/frying thermometer.

5 Using a slotted spatula, carefully slide 2 to 3 cornmeal patties into the hot oil. Cook on one side until golden, 3 to 5 minutes. Turn and cook until both sides are golden, another 3 minutes.

6 Drain on paper towels. Keep warm. Repeat until all the patties are fried.

7 When ready to serve, heat ½ inch (13 mm) of oil in a heavy skillet over medium-high heat to 375ºF (190ºC). Place the patties flat side down in the hot oil and lightly fry until crisp and golden, about 1 minute for each side. Remove from the oil, drain on paper towels, and keep warm. Repeat until all the patties are fried.

GORDITAS AND SOPES

Makes 12 gorditas or sopes

2 cups (240 g) masa harina

1 teaspoon salt

1 teaspoon regular or gluten-free baking powder (omit for sopes)

1½ (355 ml) cups water

½ cup (103 g) lard or vegetable shortening or ⅓ cup (80 ml) vegetable oil or (75 g) solid coconut oil

Vegetable oil, for frying sopes

Gorditas and sopes—two cousins of corn tortillas—are the masa delivery system for typical Mexican street snacks. They are easier to shape than tortillas because they don't have to be as thin. Basically, any filling that works with tortillas, especially corn, will be great with gorditas or sopes (pronounced *so-pez*).

On one hand, gorditas are small, puffy pastries made from leavened dough that may be patted by hand or pressed with a manual or electric tortilla press. Once formed, gorditas are toasted on a hot comal until crispy on the outside but still soft on the inside. They are usually split and filled like pita bread with roasted or stewed meats, cheese, and salsa. If you think they sound a lot like *pupusas a la El Salvador* (stuffed thick tortillas), you're right.

On the other hand, sopes are the same basic dough without leavening and a different profile. Sopes look like upside-down, mini Frisbees. With turned-up edges, sopes function like handheld tarts to hold myriad fillings, such as roasted or stewed meats, cheese, and salsa. They also may be shaped by hand or pressed with a manual press, then parbaked, shaped, and fried in hot vegetable oil.

1   Preheat a comal or griddle over medium heat to 350ºF (180ºC) or according to manufacturer's instructions if using an electric press/toaster.

2   In a large mixing bowl, combine the masa, salt, and baking powder (if using for gorditas), whisking or stirring to blend well.

3   In a small saucepan over medium heat, combine the water and lard or oil. Heat to melt the lard. Set aside off the heat to cool to lukewarm before combining with the dry ingredients.

4   Gradually add the lukewarm liquid to the dry ingredients and knead for about 3 minutes. The dough should be the consistency of Play-Doh, malleable and smooth but with enough elasticity to hold a shape.

5   Divide the dough into 12 golf ball–size rounds.

FOR GORDITAS

1   By hand, or using a press, shape the balls into ½-inch (13 mm) thick patties or gorditas, about 4 inches (10 cm) in diameter. Cover with a damp towel to prevent drying. (See page 26 for details on using a manual press or electric press/griddle. Do not press as thin as for tortillas.)

2   Lightly oil the preheated comal or griddle.

3   Toast the gorditas over medium heat for a total of 10 to 12 minutes, turning as needed to prevent overbrowning. They should puff slightly while cooking. Gorditas should cook slowly so the inside isn't too doughy. The outside should have light brown spots.

4   Allow to cool about 5 minutes for easier handling. Serve plain or split with a knife (as you would a pita or English muffin). For fillings and assembly, see Chapter 5 (page 67).

continued

continued

FOR SOPES

1 Repeat steps 1 through 5 on the previous page.

2 By hand or using an electric press, shape the balls into 12 (⅓-inch [8 mm] thick) patties or sopes. Cover with a damp towel to prevent drying. (See page 26 for details on using a manual press or electric press/griddle.) Do not press as thin as for tortillas. Sopes should be about 4 inches (10 cm) in diameter.

3 Lightly oil the preheated comal or griddle.

4 Place each sope on the oiled preheated comal or griddle and cook for about 1 minute or until the dough begins to set. Don't overcook or the dough will dry and crack. Turn and cook for another 20 to 30 seconds.

5 Using a spatula, remove the parcooked sopes from griddle. Cover the tortillas with a dry kitchen towel and cool for 30 to 45 seconds or until just cool enough to handle gingerly. Quickly—before they cool too much—turn the edges up to form a lipped edge, like a tart crust, to hold the fillings. Cover with dry towel and repeat until all the sopes are parcooked and shaped. This can be done up to 3 or 4 hours ahead.

6 When ready to serve, heat ½ inch (13 mm) of oil in a heavy skillet over medium-high heat to 375ºF (190ºC). Place the sopes flat side down in the hot oil and lightly fry until crisp and golden, about 1 minute for each side. Remove from the oil, drain on paper towels, and keep warm. Repeat until all the sopes are fried.

7 For fillings and assembly: See Chapter 5 (page 67).

HANDIWORK

When shaping gorditas and sopes, always keep a small bowl of water nearby to moisten your hands if the dough starts to stick.

BASIC FLOUR TORTILLAS

Makes 12 (6-inch [15 cm]) tortillas

2 cups (250 g) all-purpose white flour, (240 g) unbleached flour, or (240 g) finely ground whole wheat flour (or a combination)

1 teaspoon baking powder (optional)

1 teaspoon salt

½ cup (103 g) solid lard or vegetable shortening or ⅓ cup (68 g) fresh lard, (80 ml) vegetable, corn, or olive (or desired) oil, or (75 g) solid coconut oil

1 cup (235 ml) hot water (page 54 to make Flavored Flour Tortillas)

Lardy mercy, we can go on and on about the beauty of fresh flour tortillas made with lard (animal fat). The improved workability and flavor are beyond dispute. And then there's the lard renaissance movement that touts lard as better for you than shortening (vegetable fat), as long as the lard isn't hydrogenated. Most store-bought lard is, of course, hydrogenated for shelf stability.

So, you decide. It seems to me that a half-cup (103 g) of lard in a dozen homemade tortillas isn't going to be the end of you, especially if you can find unprocessed (not hydrogenated) lard, say at a farmer's market or organic/specialty/hispanic grocery.

However, the fat you choose is the fat you should use: lard, vegetable or palm oil shortening, or solid coconut oil. The fat should be at room temperature.

Note: Use less liquid oil, coconut oil, and room temperature fresh lard because these fats do not set up as firm as hydrogenated lard or shortening and don't hold a shape as well.

1   In a large bowl, stir together the flour, baking powder, and salt. Using a pastry cutter or work bowl of a food processor outfitted with a blade, cut in the lard until the mixture resembles coarse crumbs. If the mixture appears too dry, incorporate additional shortening or lard, as needed.

2   Slowly add the hot water, stirring or pulsing, to form a ball of dough. Lightly knead the dough in the bowl 30 times or as needed to form pliable, not sticky dough. Or remove the dough from the food processor work bowl and knead on a lightly floured board.

3   Place the kneaded dough in a bowl or on a pastry board. Cover with a clean kitchen towel and let rest 1 hour. This is a good stopping place if you want to serve fresh tortillas later. The dough can rest 4 to 6 hours if it is tightly covered with a layer of plastic wrap and a towel to prevent drying out. Do not refrigerate.

continued

ROUND OFF

If you REALLY want uniformly round flour tortillas, cut a paper plate the size you are obsessing over, usually 6 to 8 inches (15 to 20 cm) in diameter. Roll the tortillas as thin as you can. Lay the paper plate pattern on top and trim the edges for a "perfect" round.

continued

4 Pinch off pieces and shape the dough into 12 even-size balls. Cover with a clean kitchen towel and let rest another 20 to 30 minutes.

5 When it is time to finish the tortillas, roll each ball of dough until very thin (no thicker than the hardcover of a book, thinner if you can) using a rolling pin. Drape over the sides of a bowl and keep covered with a towel while rolling out each tortilla.

6 Cook on a hot comal or griddle (page 31). Or press and toast using an electric tortilla press/toaster (page 32).

7 Keep warm (page 33) until all the dough is used.

EXPERT ADVICE FROM SYLVIA CASARES,

author of *The Enchilada Queen Cookbook*

Flour tortillas may be parbaked (partially baked, get it?) and refrigerated up to 2 weeks. First, roll and lightly cook each tortilla on both sides, just until dough is no longer shiny. Preheat a comal or griddle to 400°F (200°C). Lightly cook the tortillas, about 1 minute on each side to set the crust. Do not cook long enough to brown or puff. Cool on a rack. Place room temperature parbaked tortillas in a plastic bag with a zipper seal. Refrigerate up to 2 weeks. When ready to cook and serve, preheat a comal or griddle. Cook on each side, about 2 to 3 minutes, or until warm with a few brown spots and slightly puffy. "These tortillas will be as tender and delicious as freshly cooked . . . as long as they aren't allowed to dry out."

GLUTEN-FREE FLOUR TORTILLAS

Makes 12 (6-inch [15 cm]) tortillas

2 cups (272 g) gluten-free flour

1 teaspoon gluten-free baking powder (optional)

1 teaspoon salt

½ cup (103 g) lard or vegetable shortening, or ⅓ cup (68 g) fresh lard, (80 ml) vegetable, corn, olive (or desired) oil, or (75 g) solid coconut oil

1 cup (235 ml) hot water

This is the basic formula using gluten-free flour. You may opt to use baking powder for fluffier tortillas. Make sure the baking powder is also gluten free. Your fat options include lard (hydrogenated or not), vegetable or palm oil shortening, or coconut oil. The fat should be at room temperature. (Flavored variations can be found on page 54 and 55.)

1 In a large bowl, stir together the flour, baking powder, and salt. Using a pastry cutter or work bowl of a food processor outfitted with a blade, cut in the lard until the mixture resembles coarse crumbs. If the mixture appears too dry, incorporate additional shortening or lard, as needed.

2 Slowly add the hot water, stirring or pulsing, to form a ball of dough. Lightly knead the dough in the bowl 30 times or as needed to form pliable, not sticky dough. Or remove the dough from the food processor work bowl and knead on a lightly floured board.

3 Place the kneaded dough in a bowl or on a pastry board. Cover with a clean kitchen towel and let rest 1 hour. This is a good stopping place if you want to serve fresh tortillas later. The dough can rest 4 to 6 hours if it is tightly covered with a layer of plastic wrap and a towel to prevent drying out. Do not refrigerate.

4 Pinch off pieces and shape the dough into 12 even-size balls. Cover with a clean kitchen towel and let rest another 20 to 30 minutes.

5 When it is time to finish the tortillas, roll each ball of dough until very thin (no thicker than the hardcover of a book, thinner if you can) using a rolling pin. Drape over the sides of a bowl and keep covered with a towel while rolling out each tortilla.

6 Cook on a hot comal or griddle (page 31). Or press and toast using an electric tortilla press/toaster (page 32).

7 Keep warm (page 33) until all the dough is used.

OF CATS AND CURES

Tortillas are the miraculous medicine in the children's book, *The Tortilla Cat*.

About Flavored Flour Tortillas

Flavoring and coloring flour tortillas is simply a matter of adding things to the basic dough. This gets trickier with gluten-free recipes because of the variations in ingredients. So, here's the deal: These flavoring recipes may require some tinkering to get the right consistency. Maybe a little more flour? Maybe a little more liquid? Once you get "the feel" for the tortilla dough of your choice, you will know how to adjust so that your flavored tortillas are soft and delicious.

Use flavored flour tortillas in any recipe for flour tortillas. Suggested uses are included.

FLAVORED FLOUR TORTILLAS

These add-ins are formulated for the Basic Flour Tortillas and Gluten-Free Flour Tortillas recipes on pages 50 and 53 that use 2 cups (250 g or 272 g) of flour. Adjust as needed to achieve the desired consistency.

For Cilantro Cumin Flour Tortillas: In a blender jar or work bowl of a food processor, combine 1 cup (16 g) of loosely packed cilantro leaves, 1 tablespoon (7 g) ground cumin or 2 tablespoons (16 g) of whole cumin seeds, and 1 cup (235 ml) of water. Process until smooth, about 1 minute. Use 1 cup (235 ml) of this liquid in the Basic Flour Tortilla recipe (page 50) or Gluten-Free Flour Tortilla recipe (page 53). If needed, add hot water to make 1 cup (235 ml).

Suggested uses: Burritos (page 140) with Spicy Chicken (page 74) or Ground Beef (page 68), with Red Posole (page 175), with Carne Guisada (Beef Stew) (page 177).

For Cilantro Lime Flour Tortillas: In a blender jar or work bowl of a food processor, combine 1 cup (16 g) of loosely packed cilantro leaves, 1 tablespoon (15 ml) of lime juice, and 1 cup (235 ml) of hot water. Process until smooth, about 1 minute. Use 1 cup (235 ml) of this liquid in the Basic Flour Tortilla recipe (page 50) or Gluten-Free Flour Tortilla recipe (page 53). If needed, add hot water to make 1 cup (235 ml).

Suggested uses: Taco Salad (page 165) with Fried Shrimp (page 76), Chicken Fajitas (page 70), with Caldo de Mariscos (Mexican Seafood Stew) (page 179).

For Nut Butter Flour Tortillas: In a small bowl, use electric beaters or a wooden spoon to combine 3 tablespoons (48 g) of creamy peanut, almond, or ground nut butter of choice with the solid fat or oil called for in the Basic Flour Tortilla recipe (page 50) or Gluten-Free Flour Tortilla recipe (page 53). Mix until well-blended. Use as directed. Optional: Add ½ teaspoon ground cinnamon to the dry ingredients and 1 tablespoon (20 g) of honey or agave nectar to the hot water. Use as directed.

Suggested uses: Flour Tortilla "Crepes" (page 191) with Pumpkin Filling (page 195) and Dulce de Leche (page 197), Cinnamon Sugar Flour Tortilla Crisps (page 193), Breakfast Burritos (page 143) with Sweet Potato Filling (page 195) and Crème Anglaise (page 196).

For Roasted Green Chile Flour Tortillas: Roast 2 large poblanos, 4 to 5 jalapeños, 6 to 8 serranos, or other desired fresh chillies (page 40) to make ½ cup (72 g) of peeled, seeded, and finely chopped roasted chillies. Place the chopped chillies and 1 cup (235 ml) of hot water in a blender container or work bowl of a food processor. Process until smooth, about 1 minute. Use 1 cup (235 ml) of this liquid in the Basic Flour Tortilla recipe (page 50) or Gluten-Free Flour Tortilla recipe (page 53). If needed, add hot water to make 1 cup (235 ml).

Suggested uses: Chimichanga (page 142) with Pork Filling (page 71), with Puerco Guisada (Red Chili Pork Stew) (page 178), with Red Posole (page 175).

For Spinach Flour Tortillas: Rinse 3 cups (90 g) of lightly packed fresh spinach in a colander; drain, but do not dry. Place the damp spinach in a medium saucepan over medium heat. Cover with a lid and cook for 3 to 5 minutes until the spinach is wilted. Transfer the spinach and cooking liquid to a blender jar or work bowl of a food processor. Process until well-blended and smooth, about 2 to 3 minutes. Use 1 cup (220 g) of pureed spinach liquid in the Basic Flour Tortilla recipe (page 50) or Gluten-Free Flour Tortilla recipe (page 53). If needed, add water to make 1 cup (235 ml).

Suggested uses: Chicken Fajitas (page 70), Breakfast Burritos (page 143), Quesadillas (page 119).

For Sriracha Flour Tortillas: Add 2 tablespoons (30 g) Sriracha to 1 cup (235 ml) hot water. Use as directed in the Basic Flour Tortilla recipe (page 50) or Gluten-Free Flour Tortilla recipe (page 53).

Suggested uses: Arizona Cheese Crisps (page 114), Mexican Street Tacos (page 130), Cheese Enchiladas (page 158) with Queso (page 99).

For Sun-Dried Tomato Flour Tortillas: In a small saucepan, combine ½ cup (28 g) sun-dried tomatoes to ¾ cup (175 ml) water. Bring to a boil; remove from the heat. Allow to cool slightly. Transfer the sun-dried tomatoes and cooking liquid to a blender jar or work bowl of a food processor. Process until well-blended and smooth, about 2 to 3 minutes. Use 1 cup (235 ml) of this liquid in the Basic Flour Tortilla recipe (page 50) or Gluten-Free Flour Tortilla recipe (page 53). If needed, add water to make 1 cup (235 ml).

Suggested uses: Baja Fish Tacos (page 132), Flour Tortilla "Noodles" Alfredo (page 182), with Chili Con Carne (page 172).

SWEET POTATO OR PUMPKIN FLOUR TORTILLAS

Makes 12 (6-inch [15 cm]) tortillas

2 cups (250 g) all-purpose white flour, (240 g) unbleached flour, or (240 g) finely ground whole wheat flour (or a combination thereof)

3 teaspoons (14 g) baking powder

1 teaspoon salt

½ cup (103 g) lard or vegetable shortening or ⅓ cup (80 ml) vegetable, corn, or olive (or desired) oil, or (75 g) solid coconut oil

¾ cup (246 g) mashed sweet potato (canned or fresh) or (184 g) pumpkin puree (canned or fresh)

½ cup (120 ml) hot water, plus additional as needed

These tortillas are particularly good with pork or chicken, or as dessert tortillas.

1   In a large bowl, stir together the flour, baking powder, and salt.

2   Using a pastry blender, fork, or two knives, mix in the lard or shortening until the flour looks like coarse crumbs.

3   Gradually add the sweet potato or pumpkin and hot water, stirring with a wooden spoon, to form a ball of dough.

4   To make the dough using a food processor outfitted with a blade, combine the dry ingredients in the work bowl. Add the lard, pulsing to combine until the mixture resembles coarse crumbs. If the mixture appears too dry, incorporate additional shortening or lard as needed. Gradually add the sweet potato or pumpkin and water, pulsing to form a ball of dough.

5   Once the dough is formed, lightly knead the dough in the bowl 30 times or as needed to form pliable, not sticky dough. Or remove the dough from the food processor work bowl and knead on a lightly floured board as above. If the dough is too sticky, add additional flour as needed.

6   Place the kneaded dough in a bowl or on a pastry board. Cover with a clean kitchen towel and let rest for 1 hour. This is a good stopping place if you want to serve fresh tortillas later. The dough can rest up to 4 to 6 hours if it is tightly covered with a layer of plastic wrap and a towel to prevent drying out. Do not refrigerate.

7   Pinch off pieces and shape the dough into 12 even-size balls. Cover with a clean kitchen towel and let rest another 20 to 30 minutes.

8   When it is time to finish the tortillas, roll each ball of dough until very thin (no thicker than the hardcover of a book, thinner if you can) using a rolling pin (page 31). Drape over the sides of a bowl and keep covered with a towel while rolling out each tortilla.

9   Cook on a hot comal or griddle (page 31). Or press and toast using an electric tortilla press/toaster (page 32).

10   Keep warm (page 33) until all the dough is used.

Suggested uses: Flour Tortilla "Crepes" (page 191), Flour Tortilla "Empanadas" (page 192), Cinnamon Sugar Flour Tortilla Crisps (page 193).

More Gluten-Free Tortillas that Use Alternative Flours

Many of us used to think "wheat" when we thought "flour." However, the past decade of gluten-free obsession has reminded us that flour means any ground grain, bean, or nut.

The following recipes use a variety of gluten-free flours. While researching the possibilities for making gluten-free tortillas, I encountered a seemingly infinite number of recipes using any and everything but flour to address an equally infinite number of allergies and dietetic concerns and guidelines.

The recipes presented here aren't intended to represent the full range and scope of possibilities for tortillas made with alternatives to wheat flour. Rather, these are the ones I found to be good. Please don't consider these options as an attempt to provide an alternative for every allergy or dietetic concern. Nor do they meet strict guidelines to be low carb/high protein, although some have those attributes. Several of these recipes call for thickeners, such as tapioca flour, or ingredients such as xanthan gum. After all, something must do the job of gluten so the dough will swell and stretch!

BLACK BEAN TORTILLAS

Makes 12 (6-inch [15 cm]) tortillas

⅓ cup (47 g) black bean flour

½ cup (64 g) cornstarch

2 tablespoons (16 g) tapioca flour

½ teaspoon salt

2 eggs, lightly beaten

1½ cup (355 ml) water

Vegetable oil spray as needed

This recipe cooks up more like crepes than tortillas. No pressing or rolling needed. Just mix, pour, and bake in a hot crepe pan or any skillet with rounded sides. This allows the batter to "crawl" up the sides, giving you a beautiful, thin black bean tortilla with very little fat. If you can't find black bean flour, make your own by using a blender to process dried black-beans into a fine-grained flour.

1 In a medium bowl, combine the black bean flour, cornstarch, tapioca flour, and salt.

2 Using a whisk, beat in the eggs and water until the batter is lump-free. The batter will be really thin. Set aside for 25 to 30 minutes to thicken.

3 Preheat a 6- or 8-inch (15 to 20 cm) crepe pan to 375°F (190°C). A pan with a nonstick surface is preferable. Or lightly coat the inside of the bottom and sides of a pan with cooking spray before cooking the tortilla.

4 When the pan is preheated, pour ¼ cup (60 ml) of batter into the pan, swirling to evenly distribute the batter and create a round, thin tortilla. Cook for 45 seconds to 1 minute or until the batter sets.

5 Using a spatula, flip the tortilla just long enough to cook the other side until light brown. Remove to a sheet of wax paper. Continue with remaining batter, separating each tortilla with a sheet of wax paper. Keep warm until ready to serve.

Suggested uses: Roll like Flour Tortilla "Crepes" (page 191) filled with Scrambled Eggs (page 136) and topped with New Mexico Red Chile Sauce (page 91).

BROWN RICE TORTILLAS

Makes 12 (6-inch [15 cm])
tortillas

1½ cups (240 g)
brown rice flour

½ cup (60 g)
tapioca flour

½ teaspoon salt

1 cup (235 ml)
boiling water

Vegetable oil
of choice

Want to go nuts over a wheat-free tortilla? Try this delicious version using nutty-tasting brown rice flour. This one tastes very similar to a corn tortilla—a double bonus if you're avoiding corn as well as gluten. Let them steam in a tortilla warmer or between two plates for 10 minutes after cooking to soften.

1 In a medium mixing bowl, whisk together the brown rice and tapioca flours and salt.

2 Using a wooden spoon, gradually mix in the boiling water to form a dough. Knead the dough in the bowl 20 times. Add water, 1 tablespoon (15 ml) at a time, if the dough feels too dry.

3 Cover with a damp towel and let rest 10 minutes.

4 Pinch off pieces and shape the dough into 12 even-size balls. Cover with a damp kitchen towel.

5 Roll each ball of dough until very thin (no thicker than the hardcover of a book, thinner if you can) using a rolling pin (page 31). Or press using a manual tortilla press (page 32). Drape over the sides of a bowl and keep covered with a damp towel while rolling out or pressing each tortilla.

6 Heat a comal or griddle over medium-high heat. When the griddle is hot enough to make a few drops of water "dance" and immediately evaporate, generously coat the hot surface with vegetable oil. Cook the tortillas 1 to 2 minutes on each side until light tan spots appear. Repeat, adding more oil as required, until all the tortillas are cooked.

7 Keep warm (page 33) until all the dough is used.

8 When all the tortillas are cooked, hold in a tortilla warmer or stack between two plates. Let sit and steam for about 10 minutes so they will be soft and pliable.

Suggested uses: Huevos Rancheros (page 148) with Green Posole (page 175), Quesadillas (page 119) filled with Grilled or Sauteed Vegetables (page 87) and Roasted Chiles (page 40).

MIXED GRAIN TORTILLAS

Makes 12 tortillas

⅔ cup (80 g) tapioca flour

⅔ cup (107 g) rice flour

⅓ cup (45 g) sorghum flour

⅓ cup (40 g) buckwheat flour

½ teaspoon gluten-free baking powder

¾ teaspoon xanthan gum

1 cup (235 ml) hot water

⅓ cup (68 g) sweet rice flour, or as needed

Vegetable oil of choice

Getting pliable, tasty wheat-free "flour" tortillas is a challenge. This is an excellent recipe; however, you probably need to be heavy into gluten-free cooking to warrant the investment in all these wheat flour alternatives. Note that the recipe calls for two kinds of rice flour. And there is a difference. "Rice flour" is made from long grain rice, whereas "sweet rice flour" is made from short grain rice (also known as sticky rice). Short grain rice has a higher starch content and is a good non-wheat alternative for thickening. I had no problem finding rice flour, but I had to use sushi (sticky) rice and grind it fine in a blender for sweet rice flour.

1 In a large bowl, combine the tapioca, rice, sorghum, and buckwheat flours, baking powder, and xanthan gum.

2 Using a wooden spoon, gradually stir in the hot water, and mix until the dough forms. If the dough is too sticky to form a ball, add sweet rice flour by the tablespoon (13 g) to achieve a soft, not sticky dough that will hold its shape.

3 Divide the dough into 12 even-size pieces. Roll to form golf ball–size orbs. Return to the bowl and cover with a damp towel.

4 Lightly sprinkle the rolling surface and a ball of dough with rice flour. Roll each ball of dough until very thin (no thicker than the hardcover of a book, thinner if you can) using a rolling pin (page 31). Or press using a manual tortilla press (page 29).

5 Heat a comal or griddle over medium-high heat. When the griddle is hot enough to make a few drops of water "dance" and immediately evaporate, generously coat the hot surface with vegetable oil.

6 When the oil is hot, slide in one tortilla. Move it about to coat the bottom with oil; flip and move it to coat that side.

7 Cook until the tortilla starts to brown, about 2 to 3 minutes. Turn and cook until the other side starts to brown, another 3 to 4 minutes. Add additional oil as needed to cook the remaining tortillas.

8 Drain on paper towels and keep warm (page 33) until all the dough is used.

Suggested uses: Quesadillas (page 119) filled with Refried Black or Pinto Beans (page 83) and favorite white or yellow cheese (page 107), Mexican Street Tacos (page 130) with Hot-Smoked Duck (page 75).

MILLET AND QUINOA TORTILLAS

Makes 12 tortillas

½ cup (60 g) millet flour

½ cup (56 g) quinoa flour

1 cup (120 g) tapioca flour

1 teaspoon gluten-free baking powder

1 teaspoon xanthan gum

1 teaspoon salt

1 tablespoon (20 g) honey or agave syrup

½ cup (120 g) warm water

4 tablespoons (103 g) shortening or lard

Want to give your tortillas a protein boost? Try these with quinoa flour—the final product is similar to a corn tortilla in texture. These tortillas also use millet, perhaps best known as birdseed. As a flour, it is good for adding a fine texture to gluten-free breads. The addition of honey or agave syrup adds a slightly sweet note to the mild, nutty flavor of the millet and quinoa. It also thickens the dough.

After baking, these tortillas also benefit from steaming in a warmer or between two plates for 5 to 10 minutes for a softer, more pliable texture. Use an electric mixer for optimum results.

1   In an electric mixer bowl or any medium-size bowl, combine the millet, quinoa, and tapioca flours, baking powder, xanthan gum, and salt. Use an electric mixer on low speed or whisk by hand to combine the dry ingredients.

2   If using an electric mixer, add the honey or agave, warm water, and shortening or lard, mixing until a dough forms around the beaters. Mix the dough on medium speed for an additional minute. Or, if going it by hand, use a wooden spoon to stir in the wet ingredients, mixing to form a soft ball. Knead 10 to 20 times. The dough will be slightly sticky and springy.

3   Wrap the dough tightly in plastic wrap and chill for 30 to 45 minutes.

4   After chilling, divide the dough into 12 equal portions, and form each into a ball. Return to bowl and cover with a damp towel to prevent drying.

5   Roll each ball of dough until very thin (no thicker than the hardcover of a book, thinner if you can) using a rolling pin (page 31). Or press using a manual tortilla press (page 29). Drape over the sides of a bowl and keep covered with a damp towel while rolling out or pressing each tortilla.

6   Heat a comal or griddle over medium-high heat. When the griddle is hot enough to make a few drops of water "dance" and immediately evaporate, generously coat the hot surface with vegetable oil. Cook the tortillas 1 to 2 minutes on each side. Repeat, adding more oil as required until all the tortillas are cooked.

7   Keep warm (page 33) until all the dough is used.

8   When all the tortillas are cooked, hold in a tortilla warmer or stack between two plates. Let sit and steam for about 10 minutes so they will be soft and pliable.

Suggested uses: Enchiladas (page 152) filled with Carnitas (page 71) topped with Real Deal Mole (page 94), or Easier Mole (page 96), Flour Tortilla "Pizza" (page 185).

GHOST TORTILLAS

Makes 12 tortillas

¾ cup (120 g) white rice flour

½ cup (60 g) tapioca flour

¼ cup (30 g) chickpea flour

½ cup (96 g) potato starch

1 teaspoon xanthan gum

1 teaspoon salt

1 teaspoon gluten-free baking powder

¼ cup (51 g) lard, shortening, or (56 g) solid coconut oil

1 cup (235 ml) hot water

This recipe produces a very white tortilla that is very similar in appearance and texture to the real thing with flour. Ground chickpeas give it a bit of a protein boost.

1   In a large bowl or work bowl of a food processor outfitted with a blade, stir together the rice, tapioca, and chickpea flours, potato starch, xanthan gum, salt, and baking powder.

2   Using a pastry cutter or food processor, cut in the lard or pulse until the mixture resembles coarse crumbs. If the mixture appears too dry, incorporate additional shortening or lard as needed.

3   Slowly add ½ cup (120 ml) of hot water, stirring or pulsing to incorporate. Gradually add the remaining water just to form a dough ball.

4   Lightly knead the dough in the bowl 20 times or as needed to form pliable, not sticky dough. Or remove the dough from the food processor work bowl and knead on a board lightly floured with rice or tapioca flour.

5   Pinch off pieces and shape the dough into 12 even-size balls. Cover with a damp kitchen towel to prevent drying out.

6   Roll each ball of dough until very thin (no thicker than the hardcover of a book, thinner if you can) using a rolling pin. Drape over the sides of a bowl and keep covered with a towel while rolling out each tortilla. Cook on a hot comal or griddle (page 31).

7   Or press and toast using an electric tortilla press/toaster (page 32).

8   Keep warm (page 33) until all the dough is used.

Suggested uses: Breakfast Tacos (page 134), Fajitas (page 70), Quesadillas (page 119).

NOW YOU'VE GOT TORTILLAS: LET'S ROLL

2 *part*

The recipes that follow use tortillas in one way or another. Dishes, like familiar rolled enchiladas (page 152), work better with thinner, more uniform, commercially-made corn tortillas that are not as fragile as homemade ones. You can use your own homemade corn tortillas for rolled enchiladas, of course, but don't say I didn't warn you. Homemade tortillas, especially flavored, make great stacked enchilada dishes.

Make the choice for homemade or store-bought this way: Is the dish more about the tortilla? Or the rest of the ingredients? If the tortilla is the star, homemade tortillas are worth the effort. If the dish is more about the filling or the sauce, it probably isn't worth your time and trouble to make and use homemade tortillas, unless you want the additional flavor complexity of flavored tortillas. But it is your time and trouble, so you decide.

In general, homemade corn tortillas (page 38) are best if eaten freshly baked and hot like rolls. Street tacos (page 130) are another happy use for homemade corn tortillas. Other dishes, like flautas (page 115) and the aforementioned enchiladas, turn out better with the uniformity, pliability, and resilience of store-bought tortillas. Still, the taste of homemade cannot be beaten.

When it comes to homemade Flour Tortillas (page 50), the same freshly baked rule applies only not quite so much. They're not as fragile and are usually more pliable than homemade corn tortillas. Fresh tortillas from your kitchen are wonderful, especially when hot with butter, like homemade bread or rolls. They also work well for Breakfast Tacos (page 134), Burritos (page 140), and Fajitas (page 70). Other dishes, such as Chimichangas (page 142), generally work better with commercially made flour tortillas. I mean, really, why stuff a homemade flour tortilla and deep fry it? Once fried, no one can tell it's homemade, and that's part of the reason to make them. So, everyone who eats one knows you made it. By hand. In your kitchen. With love.

5

FOUNDATIONS: FILLINGS, SAUCES, AND SALSAS FOR TORTILLA DISHES

Now that you have some tortillas, let's discover some great ways to use them.

Most dishes that use tortillas are ultimately assemblies that require a filling, a sauce, and garnishes. The good news for most cooks is that we can opt to make every element from scratch . . . or not.

When making fresh tortillas, some cooks may opt to use prepared sauces or fillings to streamline the process. Others may prefer to buy tortillas to use with homemade fillings and sauces.

Of course, there's the total DIY option, too. When that's the plan, get ahead of the game by making your sauce and filling in advance, if time allows. That way, when it's time to assemble the dish, making great tortillas will be your biggest challenge.

Fillings

Recipes for beef, chicken, pork, duck, and seafood fillings follow. These dishes are worth the effort. Several make enough for a couple of meals. However, when time or energy are in short supply, streamline the process by using store-bought fillings. Other shortcut options include deli roast chicken or leftover roast beef that can be seasoned to fit the tortilla profile.

GROUND BEEF FILLING

Makes about 4 cups (800 g)

2 pounds (910 g) lean ground beef, crumbled

4 tablespoons (30 g) chili powder

1 teaspoon ground cumin

½ cup (80 g) finely chopped onion

2 teaspoons finely chopped fresh garlic

1½ teaspoons salt, or to taste

1 teaspoon ground black pepper, or to taste

¾ cup (175 ml) water or beef stock

This is an all-purpose filling using ground beef. It may be used for tacos, enchiladas, burritos—whatever. You name it. It is amazingly versatile and delicious.

1 Heat a large skillet over medium-high heat. Add the ground beef and cook for 2 to 3 minutes or until the meat starts to turn gray.

2 Stir in the chili powder and ground cumin, coating the meat evenly. Cook for another 2 to 3 minutes or until the meat is no longer pink.

3 Stir in the onion, garlic, salt, and pepper. Cook until the onion is transparent, about 3 to 5 minutes longer.

4 Stir in the water and bring to a boil. Lower the heat, and simmer for 20 minutes or until most of the water is evaporated. Set aside off the heat for 10 minutes to cool.

5 Use a slotted spoon to scoop the meat from the cooking liquid for filling Tacos (page 123), Enchiladas (page 152), Burritos (page 140), Loaded Nachos (page 112), EBar Queso (page 100), or any other dish as desired.

Q: *What's the weather like in Texas?*
Chili today, hot tamale!

BEEF BRISKET FILLING AND BROTH

Makes 4 cups (800 g) meat and 3 cups (705 g) broth

4 pounds (1.8 kg) trimmed beef brisket

1 tablespoon (9 g) garlic powder

1 tablespoon (7 g) onion powder

1 tablespoon (7 g) ground cumin

2 teaspoons salt, or to taste

1 teaspoon ground black pepper, or to taste

2 to 3 bay leaves

2 cups (475 ml) beef stock or water

Shredded beef brisket is among the most flavorful fillings for tacos and nachos. Cook it until the meat shreds easily. This recipe makes enough to slice and have for dinner and then to shred for use in other dishes.

1   Preheat the oven to 350ºF (180ºC, or gas mark 4).

2   Place the beef brisket in 9 x 13-inch (23 x 33 cm) roasting pan.

3   In a small bowl or shaker, combine the garlic powder, onion powder, ground cumin, salt, and pepper. Generously coat all sides of the beef brisket with the blend, rubbing the spice blend into the meat. Let rest for 10 minutes so the spices soak into the meat.

4   Place the brisket in the oven and roast, uncovered, for 1 hour.

5   Remove the brisket from the oven. Lower the oven temperature to 300ºF (150ºC, or gas mark 2). Place 2 to 3 bay leaves in the bottom of the roasting pan. Carefully add the beef stock or water to roasting pan.

6   Tightly cover the roasting pan with heavy-duty foil. Roast for 3 to 4 hours or until the brisket is very tender. Allow to rest about 30 minutes, leaving the foil in place.

7   Using a spatula, lift the meat out of the juices. Strain the beef juices through a fine strainer. Use as au jus to moisten the brisket or for beef broth in other recipes.

8   Serve the brisket sliced against the grain, as you would pot roast. Or shred with the grain using forks or your fingers to pull the meat into shards. Use for Loaded Nachos (page 112), Tacos (page 123), or any other dish as desired.

FAJITA BEEF OR CHICKEN

Makes 4 cups (960 g)

2 pounds (910 g) beef skirt (or sirloin) steak or skinless boneless chicken breasts

½ cup (120 ml) vegetable oil, plus additional as needed

1 tablespoon (15 g) soy sauce

3 tablespoons (45 ml) lime juice

3 cloves of garlic, peeled

1 teaspoon ground cumin

1 teaspoon salt

1 teaspoon ground black pepper

½ teaspoon cayenne pepper, or to taste

Additional vegetable oil, for coating

Grilled beef or chicken strips make great fillings for flour tortillas. Known as fajitas, these juicy strips are also great in Taco Salad (page 165), Tacos (page 123), Burritos (page 140), and Chimichangas (page 142), or any other dish as desired.

Can't decide? Do a mixed grill (i.e., some of each).

The marinade in this recipe tenderizes and flavors. If preparing a mixed grill, marinate the chicken and beef separately.

Traditionally, fajitas are grilled over mesquite wood from trees indigenous to south Texas and northern Mexico. Modern fajitas may be prepared over hot coals, on a gas grill, under the oven broiler, or on the stovetop in a heavy skillet.

1   Rinse and pat the beef or chicken dry; place in a large plastic bag with zipper seal.

2   In a blender jar, combine the oil, soy sauce, lime juice, garlic, ground cumin, salt, pepper, and cayenne. Process 1 minute or until smooth.

3   Pour the marinade over the beef or chicken. Squeeze any air out of the bag, seal, and refrigerate for at least 2 hours or as long as overnight.

4   Remove the marinated beef or chicken from the refrigerator 1 hour before cooking. Drain the marinade from the beef or chicken. Pat dry with paper towels.

5   Preheat a charcoal or gas grill to medium. Or preheat the oven broiler on high. Or heat a heavy skillet, such as cast iron, over medium heat.

6   Brush the beef or chicken on all sides with vegetable oil. Lightly grease the grill, broiler pan, or heavy skillet (preferably cast iron) with additional vegetable oil.

7   Place the marinated meat or chicken on a hot grill, under a hot broiler, or in a hot skillet. Cook on one side for 3 to 4 minutes, or until brown.

8   Turn the meat and cook another 3 to 4 minutes, or until brown. Cook beef until medium rare or medium, so sliced beef will be rosy or pink when sliced. Cook chicken until the juices run clear when pierced with a fork.

9   After browning, move the chicken breasts away from hottest coals or lower the cooking temperature to medium, and cook another 5 to 7 minutes.

10 Remove meat or chicken from heat.

11 Keep warm, reserving juices.

12 Let rest 5 to 10 minutes before cutting across the grain into strips, about ¼-inch (6 mm) thick and 2 inches (5 cm) long.

BRAISED PORK AND BROTH

Makes 4 cups meat (960 g) and 3 cups (705 ml) broth.

4 pounds (1,814 g) boneless pork butt (shoulder)

2 teaspoons salt

2 teaspoons ground cumin

2 teaspoons ground black pepper

1 tablespoon (15 ml) vegetable oil

1 cup (160 g) thinly sliced onion

3 garlic cloves, peeled

1½ cups (353 ml) water

½ cup (120 ml) orange juice

3 bay leaves

2 teaspoons dried leaf Mexican oregano, marjoram, or thyme, lightly crumbled

Vegetable oil as needed for Carnitas (see below)

This juicy, flavorful pork filling starts out as a pork pot roast. Like the Beef Brisket (page 69), it can be eaten first as a roast and then shredded to make a juicy filling for Burritos (page 140) or Enchiladas (page 152), or crisped for Carnitas (below) or any dish as desired.

1 Preheat oven to 300ºF (150ºC, or gas mark 2).

2 Season the pork on all sides with salt, cumin, and black pepper.

3 In a heavy Dutch oven or other large pot over medium heat, warm the oil until it shimmers.

4 Add the pork and cook for 4 minutes or until brown. Turn and cook for 4 minutes per side until brown.

5 Add the sliced onions. Cook 5 minutes, just until the onions begin to brown around the edges. Add the garlic and cook 1 minute longer. Remove from the heat.

6 Off the heat, carefully add in the water and orange juice, stirring and scraping the bottom of the pan. Add the bay leaves and crumbled oregano, marjoram, or thyme.

7 Return to the heat and bring the liquid to a low boil.

8 When the cooking liquid simmers, cover the pan with the lid. Transfer the covered pot to oven and cook for 4 hours or until the meat falls apart.

9 Remove from the oven. Remove the lid and allow to cool for 30 minutes. Lift or spoon the meat out of juices.

10 Strain the pork juices through a fine strainer. Reserve ,and use as au jus to moisten shredded pork or as pork stock in other recipes.

11 Remove any excess fat. Serve the pork as you would pot roast. Or let cool enough to handle and use your fingers or forks to pull the meat with the grain into thin shards. Use for Loaded Nachos (page 112), Tacos (page 123) ,or Enchiladas (page 152), or any dish as desired.

FOR CARNITAS:

1 Remove any excess fat. Cut the pork into bite-size chunks. Or wait until it is cool enough to handle and use your fingers or forks to pull meat with the grain into thick shards. Cool completely.

2 Heat a large, heavy skillet over medium heat. Add just enough oil to evenly coat the bottom of the pan. Add a thin layer of pork pieces. Cook 3 to 5 minutes or until crisp on one side. Use a spatula to turn. Cook for 3 to 5 minutes or until crisp on the other side. Repeat, adding oil as necessary until all the pork is cooked crisp. Use for Loaded Nachos (page 112), Tacos (page 123), or Enchiladas (page 152), or any dish as desired.

HOMEMADE CHORIZO

Makes 4 cups (900 g)

4 cloves of garlic

1 chipotle pepper from 7-ounce (200 ml) can of chipotles in adobo sauce

1 tablespoon (3 g) dried Mexican oregano, (2 g) marjoram, or (3 g) thyme

3 tablespoons (45 ml) cider vinegar

2 tablespoons (28 ml) adobo sauce from chipotle pepper can

2 tablespoons (30 g) achiote paste, coarsely chopped

2 pounds (910 g) ground pork shoulder

6 tablespoons (45 g) chili powder

2 teaspoons salt

1 teaspoon black pepper

1 teaspoon ground allspice

Vegetable oil or cooking oil spray

Mexican-style bulk pork sausage, called chorizo, is very different from the Spanish links that are cured and dried in casings. Hispanic groceries, especially in the Southwest, stock chorizo; it is commonly found on Mexican restaurant menus, especially in breakfast dishes. If you want this flavor and can't find it to buy or simply want to make it yourself, here's an accessible recipe with very authentic taste.

The characteristic look and dried red smoky flavor of Mexican chorizo is from the addition of achiote paste, made from annatto seeds. Brick red and beautiful, this seasoning is usually found in Hispanic groceries or online. If you can't find it or don't want to bother, it is ok to eliminate the achiote. You'll have damn good fresh pork sausage.

1 In a blender jar or work bowl of a food processor, combine the garlic, chipotle, oregano, cider vinegar, adobo sauce, and achiote paste. Process 1 minute or until smooth.

2 Into a large bowl, crumble the ground pork shoulder. Add the blended mixture, chili powder, salt, black pepper, and allspice. Wearing food handler's gloves, knead the mixture by hand to evenly distribute ingredients. Or mix using a wooden spoon.

3 For the best flavor, store the chorizo overnight in a container with a tight-fitting lid.

4 To use, shape into small patties (about 3 inches [7.5 cm] in diameter by ¼-inch [6 mm] thick) or crumble and saute like ground beef. Heat a large skillet over medium heat. Lightly coat with cooking oil spray or add just enough oil to lightly coat the bottom of the pan. Cook for 5 to 7 minutes or until the pork is browned on all sides or until the patties are cooked through with no pink inside.

SPICY CHICKEN AND BROTH

Makes about 4 cups (900 g) shredded chicken and 4 cups (940 ml) broth

2 pounds (910 g) bone-in, skin-on chicken breasts and thighs

1 quart (946 ml) water or chicken stock

1 cup (160 g) thinly sliced onion

2 teaspoons salt

2 teaspoons ground cumin

2 teaspoons ground black pepper

2 bay leaves

½ cup (90 g) chopped tomato or 1¼ cup (306 g) tomato sauce

SHORTCUT SPICY SHREDDED CHICKEN OR BEEF
Makes about 3 cups (675 g)

Start with deli rotisserie chicken or pot roast. Let cool enough to handle.

- For chicken, remove the skin and discard. Shred by using your fingers to pull the white meat with the grain into thin shards. Finely chop the dark meat.

- For beef, trim any excess fat. Shred by using your fingers to pull the meat with the grain into thin shards.

Place the shredded chicken or beef in a medium saucepan over low heat. Stir in 1 tablespoon (8 g) of chili powder, stirring to coat the meat evenly. Cook for 2 to 3 minutes. Add enough water or stock to barely cover the meat. Simmer, uncovered, for 10 minutes.

Shredded chicken should be moist and flavorful. This recipe delivers in that department. For maximum juiciness, use both the white and dark meat. Or use only chicken breast. Whichever you choose, please use skin-on, bone-in chicken for rich flavor and texture. The broth can be used for soups.

1 In a large saucepan over high heat, combine the chicken and water or stock. Bring to a boil, and then reduce the heat and simmer, uncovered, for about 30 minutes.

2 Remove the chicken from the saucepan and allow to cool for about 30 minutes. Reserve the broth in the saucepan off the heat.

3 To the broth in the saucepan, add the onion, salt, cumin, black pepper, bay leaves, and chopped tomato or tomato sauce. Stir to combine.

4 When the chicken is cool enough to handle, remove the skin and discard. Using your fingers, pull the meat from the bones into thin shards or chop into bite-size pieces.

5 Over low heat, add the chicken to the broth mixture. Simmer for 20 minutes or until soft.

6 Set aside off the heat for about 15 minutes to cool. Using a slotted spoon, transfer the seasoned chicken meat to a clean container, draining most of the liquid. Strain the cooking liquid through a fine strainer and reserve for broth.

ROAST DUCK

Makes 4 cups (900 g)

1 (5- to 6-pound [2.3 to 2.7 kg]) duck

Boiling water

1½ tablespoons (27 g) salt

2 teaspoons ground black pepper

1 teaspoon cayenne pepper or smoked paprika

DUCK FAT FLOUR TORTILLAS

Why not? We love French fries crisped in duck fat. Why wouldn't we love tortillas made from that same rich-flavored fat? Reserve fat from duck roasting pan and pour through a fine strainer to eliminate solids. Use ⅓ cup (67 g) duck fat to make Basic Flour Tortillas, page 50.

Roasting a duck is almost as easy as roasting a chicken. Duck may also be hot-smoked on a grill over indirect heat. Crispy skin is the best part so be sure and chop some for adding to the duck meat.

1 Remove the neck and giblets. Discard or use to make stock. Using a sharp fork, prick the skin on all sides. Do not pierce the meat under the layer of fat and skin.

2 Trim off any loose skin and excess fat. Place the trimmed skin and fat in a single layer in an ovenproof skillet or small, shallow baking pan.

3 Combine the salt, black pepper, and cayenne or paprika. Lightly sprinkle the duck skin in the skillet with the spice mixture. Rub the duck inside and out with the remaining seasoning blend.

4 Heat the oven to 425°F (220°C, or gas mark 7). Place the duck on a rack in a roasting pan breast side up. Place the roasting pan with the duck and the skillet with the fat and skin in the hot oven for 15 minutes.

5 Lower the oven to 350°F (180°C, or gas mark 4).

6 For the duck skin and fat turn the pieces after 20 minutes. Cook an additional 5 to 10 minutes, or until brown and crisp. Remove the skin from the oven and drain on paper towels; reserve.

7 For the duck, remove the roasting pan from the oven after 45 minutes. Turn the duck breast-side down on the rack in roasting pan. Return to oven for 30 minutes.

8 Remove the roasting pan from the oven. Turn the duck breast-side up on the rack in the roasting pan. Return to the oven for 15 to 30 minutes, or until the skin is crisp and a meat thermometer inserted in the thigh registers 175°F (80°C). Cooking time should be about 22 minutes per pound.

9 Let the duck rest at least 15 minutes. Slice and carve to serve, or allow to cool completely. Use your fingers to pull off the skin. Cut the meat from the bones and tear it into shreds. Rough chop pieces of crisp skin to mix with the meat.

10 Use as filling for Tacos (page 123), Loaded Nachos (page 112), or any dish as desired.

HOT-SMOKED DUCK

1 Follow Steps 1 through 3 above.

2 Heat a charcoal or gas grill to medium high.

3 Place the duck on an oiled grill, not directly over hot coals or heat source. Lower the lid of the cooker and hot smoke the duck for 1½ to 2 hours, or until a meat thermometer inserted in the thigh registers 175°F (80°C), about 22 minutes per pound (455 g).

4 To crisp trimmed skin and fat, place in the oven at 350°F (180°C, or gas mark 4) for 30 minutes.

SHRIMP OR CRAB

Makes about 2 cups (450 g)

1 pound (455 g) medium shrimp, peeled and deveined; or lump crabmeat, picked over to remove any pieces of shell

2 cloves of garlic, finely chopped

2 tablespoons (28 ml) lime juice

1 tablespoon (14 g) unsalted butter or (15 ml) olive oil, or a combination

½ teaspoon salt, or to taste

Succulent seafood is a great complement to fresh tortillas. Truly fresh shrimp or lump crab, simply sautéed or broiled, makes a great filling for enchiladas or tacos—or on top of a chalupa, mounded with guacamole and pico de gallo.

1 The shrimp may be prepared whole or cut into 3 pieces for stuffing into tacos or enchiladas. In a medium bowl, toss together the shrimp or crabmeat with the garlic and lime juice.

2 In a medium skillet over medium heat, melt the butter or heat the oil. Add the shrimp (or crabmeat) and cook, stirring constantly, for 2 minutes or until the shrimp are just pink and the crabmeat is heated through. Season with salt.

3 Use to fill Tacos (page 123), Enchiladas (page 152), top Loaded Nachos (page 112), or Chalupas (page 116), or any dish as desired.

FRIED SHRIMP

Makes 2 cups (450 g)

1 pound (455 g) medium shrimp, peeled and deveined

1 cup (125 g) all-purpose or (120 g) unbleached flour

1 teaspoon salt

¼ teaspoon cayenne pepper

1 egg, lightly beaten

½ cup (115 ml) milk

2 cups (224 g) panko bread crumbs or (275 g) yellow cornmeal

Vegetable oil, for frying

Lemon or lime wedges

This recipe makes great fried shrimp as an entrée or as a filling for any tortilla dish that combines well with seafood. Instead of traditional lettuce garnish, consider a Creamy, Spicy, Maybe Sweet Slaw (page 88).

1 The shrimp may be fried whole or cut into 2 pieces.

2 Place the flour, salt, and cayenne in a shallow bowl. Mix well.

3 In another shallow bowl, whisk together the egg and milk.

4 Place the panko or cornmeal in the bottom of a third shallow bowl.

5 Add the oil to an electric skillet and heat to 375ºF (190ºC). Or in a heavy skillet over medium-high heat, add an inch (2.5 cm) of oil and heat to 375ºF (190ºC).

6 Place several shrimp or a handful of pieces of shrimp into the flour, turning to coat evenly.

7 Shake off any excess flour and drop the shrimp into the egg-milk mixture. Use a slotted spoon to transfer the shrimp to the panko or cornmeal, turning to coat evenly and completely.

8 Place the shrimp in the hot oil and fry about 1 minute on each side or until golden brown.

9 Drain on paper towels. Keep warm.

10 Repeat until all the shrimp are fried.

11 Use to fill Tacos (page 123) or top Chalupas (page 116), or on any dish as desired. Serve with lemon or lime wedges to squeeze on the shrimp.

GRILLED OR BROILED FISH

Makes 2 cups (450 g)

1 pound (455 g) skinless fillets of white fish such as mahi mahi, halibut, cod, tilapia, or catfish

½ cup (80 g) thinly sliced onion

¼ cup (4 g) coarse chopped fresh cilantro leaves

½ cup (120 ml) olive or vegetable oil

3 tablespoons (45 ml) lime juice

3 tablespoons (45 ml) orange juice

1 teaspoon dried Mexican oregano

1 teaspoon garlic seasoning blend

1 teaspoon ground black pepper, or to taste

Do you love fish tacos but want to skip the deep-frying? Try grilling or broiling any firm-fleshed, white fish. Break the fish into chunks and use to fill tacos along with Creamy, Spicy, Maybe Sweet Slaw (page 88).

1 Rinse the fish fillets and pat dry.

2 In a 2-cup (475 ml) measure, combine the onion, cilantro, oil, lime and orange juices, and oregano.

3 Sprinkle the fish on both sides with the garlic seasoning blend and black pepper. Place the fish in a glass baking dish large enough to hold the fish in a single layer.

4 Spoon the onion mixture over the fish. Turn the fish to coat both sides, spooning additional marinade over top.

5 Cover and chill for 30 minutes to 1 hour.

6 Meanwhile, heat the charcoal or gas grill to medium high. Or preheat the oven to 375ºF (190ºC, or gas mark 5).

7 After the fish has marinated, shake off most of the marinade. Place on the oiled grate and grill 3 to 5 minutes on each side or until opaque and flaky. Or bake in single layer in a 9 x 13-inch (23 x 33 cm) glass baking dish sprayed with cooking oil. Bake 7 to 10 minutes or until opaque and flaky.

8 Coarsely chop the cooked fish for Tacos (page 125 to 132), Chalupas (page 116), or any dish as desired.

BEER BATTER FRIED FISH

Makes 2 cups (450 g)

1 pound (455 g) firm flesh white fish fillets, such as mahi mahi, halibut, cod, tilapia, or catfish

1½ cups (188 g) all-purpose or (180 g) unbleached flour, divided use

¼ cup (32 g) cornstarch

1 teaspoon salt

1 teaspoon pepper

1 teaspoon baking powder

¼ teaspoon cayenne pepper

1 cup (235 ml) beer

1 egg, lightly beaten

Vegetable oil, for frying

Lime or lemon wedges

Crispy beer batter-fried fish is the gold standard for Baja California–style fish tacos. This simple batter works great. Use a firm fleshed white fish.

1 Rinse the fish and pat dry. Cut the fish into 1 x 2-inch (2.5 x 5 cm) strips.

2 In a medium bowl, whisk together ¾ cup (94 g) of flour, cornstarch, salt, pepper, baking powder, and cayenne.

3 Whisk the beer and egg into the flour mixture, stirring until combined but still slightly lumpy. Do not overmix.

4 Line the bottom of a shallow bowl with ¾ cup (94 g) of flour.

5 In a heavy skillet over medium heat, add 1 inch (2.5 cm) of oil. Heat to 375ºF (190ºC).

6 When the oil is hot, dip 4 or 5 pieces of fish in the flour. Shake off any excess and then dip into the beer batter. Allow any excess to drip off.

7 Fry the fish in the hot oil until golden, about 1 to 2 minutes on each side, turning once.

8 Drain on paper towel–lined plate. Keep warm.

9 Repeat until all the shrimp are fried.

10 Use for Tacos (page 123), Chalupas (page 116), or any dish as desired. Serve with lemon or lime wedges to squeeze on the fish.

FILLED WITH LUTEFISK?

Norway and Sweden account for 40 percent of Europe's taco consumption.

Sides and More Fillings

This section of the book includes recipes that do double duty. Dishes like beans, rice, and grilled vegetables may be used as fillings for tacos, burritos, or enchiladas or as sides.

BEANS

Beans are the classic tortilla go-with—and not just because they taste good. Beans, both pinto and black, are the natural partner with tortillas and rice because the combination makes for an inexpensive source of protein. Combining corn or rice with beans adds up to the nine essential amino acids for a complete protein.

You can start with dried beans for authenticity and economy. Stew them and then mash and reheat to make what are called "refried beans." Who knows why? They're "fried," meaning reheated, only once.

Or, you can take a shortcut (which is perfectly acceptable) and start with canned beans to then mash and reheat to make "refried beans." Heck, you can even open a can or package of refried beans, add a little flavor, and you're in business.

Pinto (never red) and black beans are the more authentic choices for Latin dishes. Red beans are for Cajun red beans and rice. Kidney beans belong on the shelf.

Pinto Beans

Reddish brown beans, known as pinto beans, are the foundation of a great many tortilla-based dishes, especially in Mexico and the Southwest.

BASIC, FROM SCRATCH, PINTO BEANS

Makes about 6 cups (1 kg)

2 cups (384 g) dry pinto beans

5 cups (1.2 L) water, chicken, pork, or vegetable stock

1 cup (160 g) chopped yellow or white onions

2 cloves of garlic, finely chopped

1 fresh epazote sprig (optional) or 2 bay leaves

1 dried chile de arbol or ¼ teaspoon cayenne pepper

2 teaspoons cumin

1½ teaspoons salt, or to taste

1 teaspoon ground black pepper, or to taste

Start with a bag of dried beans, add liquid and seasonings, simmer, simmer, simmer, and enjoy. This recipe is also the basis for pinto bean soup and refried pinto beans.

1. Pick through the beans to remove any impurities or shriveled beans. Place in a large bowl with enough water to cover. Remove any beans that float. Pour the beans and water into a colander to drain. Rinse the beans thoroughly with cold water.

2. In a large saucepan over high heat, combine the water or chicken, pork, or vegetable stock, beans, onions, garlic, epazote sprig or bay leaves, dried chilli or cayenne, and cumin. Bring to a boil and then reduce the heat, cover, and simmer for about 2 to 3 hours or until the beans are soft.

3. The ingredients also may be combined and cooked in a slow cooker for 4 to 5 hours or until the beans are soft.

4. When the beans are tender, add the salt and pepper. Adjust the seasoning to taste. Remove the epazote sprig or bay leaves berfore serving.

BASIC, FROM SCRATCH, BLACK BEANS

Makes about 6 cups (1 kg)
(12 servings)

2 cups (360 g) dry black beans

5 cups (1.2 L) water or chicken, pork, or vegetable stock

1 cup (160 g) chopped yellow or white onion

2 cloves of garlic, finely chopped

1 fresh epazote sprig (optional) or 2 bay leaves

1 dried chilli arbol or ¼ teaspoon cayenne pepper

1½ teaspoons salt, or to taste

Black beans are used more often in Latin America than in Mexico. They are traditional, especially in California, with many seafood dishes that use tortillas, such as Baja California-style fish tacos. This recipe is also the basis for black bean soup and refried black beans.

An optional ingredient in this dish is the epazote sprig. This dried herb can be found in many Hispanic markets. Besides producing a deep earthy flavor, epazote moderates the gassy effect of beans.

1 Pick through the beans to remove any impurities or shriveled beans. Place in a large bowl with enough water to cover. Remove any beans that float. Pour the beans and water into a colander to drain. Rinse the beans thoroughly with cold water.

2 In a large saucepan over high heat, combine the water or chicken, pork, or vegetable stock, beans, onions, garlic, epazote or bay leaves, and dried chilli or cayenne. Bring to a boil and then reduce the heat, cover, and simmer for about 2 to 3 hours or until the beans are soft.

3 The ingredients also may be combined and cooked in a slow cooker for 4 to 5 hours or until the beans are soft.

4 When the beans are tender, add the salt. Adjust the seasoning to taste. Remove the epazote sprig or bay leaves berfore serving.

REFRIED PINTO OR BLACK BEANS

Makes about 3 cups (516 g)

3 cups (516 g) Basic, From Scratch, Pinto or Black Beans (page 80 or 81), drained, liquid reserved

¼ cup (51 g) lard or (60 ml) vegetable oil

¼ cup (40 g) finely chopped onions

2 cloves of garlic, finely chopped

Satiny smooth consistency is what makes refried beans so delicious, like very creamy mashed potatoes. Achieving this can be done with a blender or food processor and the right amount of liquid.

1   In a blender jar or work bowl of a food processor, process or mash the beans (in 2 or 3 batches) until they are smooth, adding a small amount of cooking liquid, as needed.

2   In a large skillet over medium-high heat, melt the lard or heat the oil until it shimmers. Add the onions and cook for about 3 minutes, stirring frequently, until soft but not brown. Add the garlic and cook for another minute.

3   Stir the mashed beans into the onions and lower the heat. Simmer for another 10 minutes, stirring occasionally.

4   If needed, thin the beans with some of the reserved cooking liquid. Adjust the seasoning to taste. The beans should be spoonable, like creamy whipped potatoes.

REFRIED BEANS FROM CANNED PINTO OR BLACK BEANS

Makes about 3 cups (516 g)

2 cans (14½ ounces, or [410 g]) of pinto or black beans, undrained

¼ cup (60 ml) vegetable oil

½ cup (80 g) chopped white or yellow onion

2 cloves of garlic, finely chopped

¼ teaspoon salt, or to taste

⅛ teaspoon cayenne pepper, or to taste

This shortcut recipe works with pinto or black beans. By using canned beans, you save yourself the long simmer time required to hydrate and soften dried beans.

1   In a blender jar or work bowl of a food processor, process the beans until well-blended and smooth. Set aside.

2   In a large skillet over medium-high heat, warm the oil until it shimmers. Add the onions and cook for about 3 minutes, stirring frequently, until soft but not brown. Add the garlic and cook for another couple of minutes.

3   Stir the mashed beans into the onions and lower the heat. Simmer for another 10 minutes, stirring occasionally. If needed, thin the beans with enough water or stock to achieve the desired consistency. Adjust the seasoning to taste. The beans should be spoonable, like creamy mashed potatoes.

4   Serve hot.

Rice

When it comes to tortilla cuisines, corn tortillas, "red rice," and pinto beans are usually served together. Likewise, flour tortillas, "green rice," and black beans are the more traditional combo. That doesn't mean you can't mix and match according to what you like.

Often called "Mexican rice," red rice gets its color from its cooking liquid, which includes tomato sauce or chopped tomatoes. Green rice starts with the same base—long-grain white rice—and gets its color from chopped herbs and chiles.

Both are cooked like pilaf—sautéed in oil before liquid is added. This technique keeps the grains firm and prevents clumping.

RED RICE

Makes 6 servings (1.1 kg)

2 tablespoons (28 ml) vegetable oil

1 cup (185 g) long-grain white rice

½ cup (90 g) chopped tomato

½ cup (80 g) finely chopped white or yellow onion

2 cloves of garlic, finely chopped

1 teaspoon ground cumin

½ teaspoon ground black pepper

2¼ cups (535 ml) water or Spicy Chicken Broth (page 74)

3 tablespoons (46 g) tomato sauce

1 teaspoon salt

1 cup (140 g) frozen (rinsed with hot water and drained) peas and carrots (optional)

This recipe represents the traditional look and flavor of Tex-Mex rice. There's an old-school option—the addition of peas and chopped carrots—that can add color contrast.

1 In a large skillet over medium heat, warm the oil until it shimmers. Add the rice and cook, stirring frequently, for 3 to 5 minutes, until the rice turns a golden brown.

2 Add the tomato, onion, garlic, cumin, and black pepper. Stir and cook for 3 minutes or until the onions are soft. Remove from the heat.

3 Stirring constantly, carefully add the water or broth, tomato sauce, and salt. Return to the heat, and bring to a boil over high heat.

4 Reduce the heat, cover, and simmer for 15 minutes or until the liquid is absorbed and the rice is tender. Set aside off the heat, covered, for 5 minutes. Fluff the rice with a fork. Stir in the peas and carrots, if using.

GREEN RICE

Makes 6 servings (1.1 kg)

2 tablespoons (26 g) lard or vegetable oil (28 ml)

1 cup (185 g) long-grain white rice

1 cup (150 g) chopped fresh poblano chile (seeds removed) or ½ cup (72 g) canned or roasted green or poblano chile (page 40)

½ cup (80 g) finely chopped white or yellow onion

2 cloves of garlic, finely chopped

½ teaspoon ground black pepper

2¼ cups (535 ml) water or Spicy Chicken Broth (page 74)

1 teaspoon salt

½ cup coarsely (8 g) chopped cilantro leaves

1 cup (165 g) frozen corn (rinsed with hot water and drained) or (154 g) fresh corn off the cob (optional)

The addition of green chillies and cilantro gives this rice a gentle piquancy and beautiful color. For more color, add some corn.

1 In a large skillet over medium heat, warm the oil until it shimmers. Add the rice and cook, stirring frequently, for 3 to 5 minutes, until the rice turns a golden brown.

2 Add the chiles, onion, garlic, and black pepper. Stir and cook 3 minutes or until the onions are soft. Remove from the heat.

3 While stirring constantly, carefully add the water or broth, and salt. Return to the heat and bring to a boil over high heat.

4 Reduce the heat, cover, and simmer for 15 minutes or until the liquid is absorbed and the rice is tender. Set aside off the heat, covered, for 5 minutes. Fluff the rice with a fork. Stir in the cilantro and corn, if using.

Vegetables

Play around with the vegetables you use for these dishes. Adding vegetables to a tortilla dish is also an opportunity to add some color.

GRILLED OR SAUTÉED VEGETABLES

Makes 4 cups (455 g)

4 cups coarsely chopped (squash [560 g], spinach [120 g], eggplant [328 g], tomatoes [720 g]) or sliced (chile or green peppers [600 g], onions [640 g], mushrooms [280 g]), or other vegetables, as desired

1 tablespoon (15 ml) vegetable oil

1½ teaspoons garlic seasoning blend or salt, or to taste

1 teaspoon pepper, or to taste

Whether you are grilling onions and green peppers for fajitas, or a mixture of spinach and mushrooms for filling enchiladas, or a combination of squash and chillies as a side dish, grilled veggies are an important part of the tortilla sidekick repertoire.

1   In a large skillet or a griddle over medium heat, warm the oil until it shimmers.

2   Add the vegetables. Cook, stirring frequently, for 5 minutes or until the onion or peppers are tender and brown at the edges. Season with the garlic seasoning blend or salt and pepper to taste, mixing well.

3   Cover and set aside off heat for 5 minutes before serving.

CREAMY, SPICY, MAYBE SWEET SLAW

Makes 4 cups (400 g)

3 cups (210 g) coarsely shredded green or (225 g) Napa cabbage

¾ cup (120 g) finely chopped red, yellow, or white onion, rinsed and drained

¼ cup (4 g) chopped fresh cilantro leaves

1 cup (155 g) chopped fresh pineapple or (175 g) mango (optional)

¼ cup (60 g) plain Greek yogurt

¼ cup (60 g) mayonnaise

1 tablespoon (15 ml) lime juice

1 teaspoon salt, or to taste

½ teaspoon ground black pepper, or to taste

⅛ teaspoon cayenne pepper, or to taste

Whether you serve this dish as a side or a garnish for shrimp or fish tacos, it is reliable and easy to put together. Use green cabbage or Napa cabbage. Red, yellow, or white onion is another option and an opportunity to add some color. If you want a sweet and spicy flavor contrast, add pineapple or mango.

1 In a large bowl, combine the cabbage, onion, cilantro, and pineapple or mango, if using.

2 In a small bowl, blend the yogurt, mayonnaise, lime juice, salt, black pepper, and cayenne. Stir until smooth.

3 Pour the blended yogurt and mayonnaise over the cabbage mixture. Stir to evenly coat the vegetables.

4 Refrigerate for at least 1 hour before serving.

Sauces, Salsas, and Dips

The recipes in this section are for a variety of sauces and salsas with an affinity for tortillas. Let's start with those that go well with enchiladas and other main dishes, like burritos. From there, we'll roll out a variety of dipping and garnishing sauces.

TEX-MEX CHILI GRAVY

Makes 3 cups (825 g)

2 cups (475 ml) Beef Broth (page 69), or store-bought

¼ cup (56 g) packed ground beef, crumbled

¼ cup (60 ml) vegetable oil

¼ cup (31 g) all-purpose or (30 g) unbleached flour

¼ cup (30 g) chili powder

2 teaspoons granulated garlic or garlic powder

2 teaspoons ground cumin

1 teaspoon salt, or to taste

1 teaspoon ground black pepper

This is the iconic sauce for Tex-Mex enchiladas. Ladled over cheese enchiladas, this is the stuff that makes believers out of skeptics. The addition of a small amount of ground beef gives the sauce additional body and flavor without turning it into the meaty stew known as *Chili con Carne* (page 172). The color is a dark, reddish brown.

Mexican-Americans call this "gravy" in the same way that Italian-Americans refer to spaghetti sauce as "gravy." It has the characteristic Tex-Mex flavor imparted by cumin, which is the distinctive aroma in chili powder.

Note: For quicker chili gravy, omit ground beef. Begin with step 3 below and proceed as directed. Simmer 10 minutes or until thickened.

1 In a small saucepan over medium heat, combine the Beef Broth and crumbled ground beef. Bring to a boil. Reduce the heat and simmer for 10 minutes. Use a large, shallow spoon to skim any gray foam that floats to the surface and accumulates around the edge of the pan; discard.

2 Using the back of a large, shallow spoon, press any chunks of beef against the side of the pan to separate and smooth the meat into the broth. Reserve off the heat.

3 In large skillet over medium heat, whisk together the oil and flour. Stir continually until the mixture is bubbly and smooth. Cook for 5 minutes or until flour begins to turn a light brown, about the color of café au lait.

4 Whisk in the chili powder, garlic, cumin, salt, and pepper, stirring until smooth. Cook for another 2 minutes.

5 Slowly and carefully add the reserved beef broth and beef, about ½ cup (120 ml) at a time, stirring constantly. When all the broth is added, stir and cook until the "gravy" is smooth. Reduce the heat to low and simmer for 20 minutes.

NEW MEXICO RED CHILE SAUCE

Makes 3 cups (825 g)

6 ounces (170 g) (about 15) whole dried red ancho or New Mexican chillies, stems and seeds removed, rinsed well

2 teaspoons dried Mexican oregano or marjoram

1½ cups (355 ml) water

2 tablespoons (28 ml) vegetable oil

1 cup (160 g) chopped white or yellow onion

3 cloves of garlic, finely chopped

1 teaspoon salt, or to taste

1½ cups (355 ml) Spicy Chicken Broth (page 74) or water

While Tex-Mex Chili Gravy is distinctly Tex-Mex, this particular sauce is an exquisite culinary expression of New Mexico using ancho chiles, the name for dried poblano peppers. Compared to Chili Gravy, the flavor of this enchilada sauce is almost pure red chile, lightly enhanced by onion, garlic, and Mexican oregano.

1 In a medium saucepan over medium heat, combine the red chiles, dried oregano, and water. Bring to a boil, reduce the heat, and simmer for 15 minutes. Set aside off the heat for 10 minutes to cool.

2 In a blender jar or the work bowl of a food processor, process the red chile mixture until smooth, about 2 to 3 minutes.

3 Pour the processed chile mixture through a fine strainer into a small bowl, pressing with the back of a spoon to push as much liquid and smooth pulp into the bowl as possible; set aside. Discard the remaining skins.

4 In a medium saucepan over medium heat, heat the oil until it shimmers.

5 Stir in the onion and cook, stirring frequently, until the onion is soft but not brown, about 3 minutes. Add the garlic and cook for 1 minute longer, stirring constantly.

6 Add the processed chile mixture, salt, and Spicy Chicken Broth or additional water. Reduce the heat and simmer for 20 minutes.

7 The sauce should cook down and be thick enough to coat the back of a spoon. Set aside off the heat for 10 minutes to further thicken.

TOMATO AND GREEN CHILE SAUCE

Makes about 3 cups (735 g)

7 tomatoes (about 3 pounds [1.4 kg] total), coarsely chopped or 2 cans (28 ounces, or 785 g each) of diced tomatoes, undrained

2½ cups (590 ml) water

3 tablespoons (45 ml) vegetable oil

1 cup (160 g) chopped white or yellow onion

3 fresh jalapeños, stems removed and seeds removed if desired, finely chopped; or 3 fresh green New Mexico or Anaheim green chiles, stems removed, finely chopped; or 1 cup (50 ml) chopped canned or (144 g) roasted green chiles, drained

2 cloves of garlic, finely chopped

1½ teaspoons salt, or to taste

1 teaspoon ground black pepper, or to taste

½ cup (123 g) tomato sauce (optional)

Made with tomatoes and chiles, this vegetarian sauce has vibrant flavor and color, especially if you can find fresh, vine-ripened tomatoes to complement the chiles. This is the sauce for you if you grow your own tomatoes and chiles. In the off-season, canned whole peeled tomatoes will do just fine. So will chiles from the produce aisle.

Remember to use plastic food handlers' gloves when handling fresh chilli peppers to protect your hands, eyes, nose, and lips. Do not to touch your face with gloved hands that have handled fresh chile peppers.

Even with fresh jalapeños, this sauce is relatively mild. For even less heat, remove the seeds from jalapeños or use milder New Mexico green or Anaheim chiles. Want something even milder? Use roasted chiles (page 40).

1   In a medium saucepan over high heat, combine the fresh tomatoes with the water. Bring to a boil and then reduce the heat and simmer for 20 minutes. Set aside, off the heat, to cool slightly.

2   If using canned tomatoes, transfer the undrained tomatoes to a 3-cup measure (700 ml), and add enough water to fill.

3   In a large saucepan over medium heat, warm the oil until it shimmers. Add the onion, chiles, and garlic; cook for 5 minutes or until the onions are soft.

4   Add the cooked or canned tomatoes to the onion mixture, along with the salt and pepper. If a deeper red color is desired, add ½ cup (123 g) of tomato sauce.

5   Reduce the heat and simmer for 8 to 10 minutes. Set aside, off the heat, for at least 10 minutes to let the flavors mellow before serving.

GREEN TOMATILLO SAUCE

Makes about 3 cups (735 g)

1½ pounds (680 g) tomatillos, rinsed after peeling papery outer skin, cut in half

1 large white or yellow onion, peeled, stem end removed, and cut into 4 pieces

3 serrano chillies, stems removed (no need to remove seeds)

1 small tomato, cored and cut into 4 pieces

2½ cups (570 ml) Spicy Chicken Broth (page 74) or water, divided use

3 cloves of garlic

½ cup (8 g) cilantro leaves

1¼ teaspoons salt

Don't reserve this sauce for enchiladas only, although it is *the* traditional sauce for Chicken Enchiladas (page 156). Green Tomatillo Sauce is also the one to use for Chilaqiles (page 146) and is a great vegetarian sauce if made without chicken stock. Tomatillos are the "green" in this sauce. They look like small green tomatoes with papery outer skins at the stem end. The roasted version is delicious as well.

1   In a large saucepan over medium heat, combine the tomatillos, onion, chillies, tomato, and 2 cups (475 ml) of Spicy Chicken Broth or water. Bring to a boil and then lower the heat and simmer for 20 minutes or until all the ingredients are very soft. Set aside off the heat to cool, about 10 minutes.

2   In a blender jar or work bowl of a food processor, process the garlic, cilantro, and salt with ½ cup (120 ml) of Spicy Chicken Broth or water until smooth, about 1 minute.

3   Add the tomatillo mixture. Process on high speed until very smooth, about 2 minutes, or less if a chunkier sauce is desired.

4   Return to the saucepan and simmer on very low heat for 5 minutes. The sauce should be the consistency of thick salsa. If needed, simmer 5 minutes longer or until thickened to the desired consistency.

FOR ROASTED TOMATILLO SAUCE

1   Preheat the broiler.

2   On a rimmed baking sheet or sheet pan lined with foil, arrange the tomatillos, onion, and tomato. Place on a high rack directly under the broiler for 4 to 5 minutes or until the tomatillos blister and start to turn black. Turn all the vegetables and broil on the other side another 3 to 4 minutes or until blackened and softened.

3   Remove from the oven and let cool enough to handle, about 10 minutes. In a blender jar or work bowl of a food processor, process the garlic, cilantro, and salt with ½ cup (120 ml) of Spicy Chicken Broth or water about 1 minute.

4   Add the roasted vegetables to the blender, along with pan juices and 1 cup (235 ml) of Spicy Chicken Broth or water. Process on high speed until very smooth, about 2 minutes, or less if a chunkier sauce is desired. If the sauce is too thick, add more water or Spicy Chicken Broth.

5   Return to the saucepan and reheat gently.

REAL DEAL MOLE

Makes about 4 cups (1 kg)

6 guajillo chiles, stems and seeds removed

4 ancho chiles, stems and seeds removed

2 pasilla chiles, stems and seeds removed

3 cups (700 ml) Spicy Chicken Broth (page 74) or water, divided use

½ cup (80 g) chopped white onion

2 cloves of garlic

½ cup (72 g) sesame seeds

½ teaspoon anise seeds

¼ teaspoon coriander seeds

6 tablespoons (90 ml) vegetable oil, preferably peanut oil

2 corn tortillas (6 inches, or 15 cm), torn into pieces to make about 1 cup

¼ cup (35 g) dark raisins

¼ cup (36 g) whole blanched almonds

¼ cup (35 g) hulled pumpkin seeds, unsalted

1 Mexican chocolate tablet (3.1 ounces, or 87 g), or 3 ounces (85 g) semisweet chocolate, broken into small pieces

5 teaspoons (27 g) peanut butter

2 teaspoons cinnamon

1 teaspoon ground cloves

1 teaspoon salt

1 teaspoon cayenne pepper, or to taste

½ teaspoon agave syrup, or to taste

Yeah, this sauce is a project. If you want a shortcut version, see page 96. If you decide to take the mole challenge, I swear that the result is worth the effort. Besides, as much work as this is, imagine what it would be like to grind chiles, seeds, nuts, and chocolate to make mole like the Indians did—on a grinding stone, without a blender or food processor. Now that's real work! The traditional chocolate used in mole is the tablet form of coarse Mexican chocolate, which is used for making hot chocolate. Nestlé Chocolate Abuelita is a common and favorite brand. But your favorite semisweet chocolate will also do.

1 In a medium saucepan over low heat, combine the chiles and 2 cups (475 ml) of Spicy Chicken Broth or water. Bring to a boil and then lower the heat and simmer for 15 minutes. Set aside off the heat to cool for 15 minutes.

2 In a blender jar or a food processor work bowl, process the chiles and their cooking liquid for 1 minute or until smooth and the chiles are liquefied.

3 Pour the pureed chile mixture through a fine strainer into a small bowl, pressing with the back of a spoon to extract as much liquid and smooth pulp as possible; set aside. Discard the solids.

4 Return the chile puree to blender or work bowl of a food processor. Add the onions and garlic. Process until smooth, about 2 minutes. Reserve.

5 In a large, dry skillet over medium heat, toast the sesame, anise, and coriander seeds, tossing frequently, about 3 minutes or until the sesame seeds are golden. Add the toasted seeds to the blender or work bowl of a food processor.

6 In the same skillet over medium heat, warm the oil until it shimmers. Add the tortilla pieces, raisins, almonds, and pumpkin seeds. Stir and cook for about 2 minutes or until the tortillas and seeds are light brown. Cool slightly. Add the contents of the skillet, including the oil, to a blender jar or work bowl of food processor. Process for 2 minutes or until smooth.

7 In the same medium saucepan over low heat, warm 1 cup (120 ml) of Spicy Chicken Broth or water. Add the chocolate, stirring constantly, until melted and blended to a smooth consistency. Using a whisk or an immersion blender, stir in peanut butter, cinnamon, cloves, salt, cayenne, and agave syrup; blend until smooth. Set aside off the heat to cool slightly.

8 Add the chocolate-peanut butter mixture to a blender jar or work bowl of a food processor. Process for 2 minutes until the sauce is smooth.

9 Transfer the blended mixture to the large skillet over low heat. Simmer for 10 minutes or until the sauce is the consistency of ketchup. To thin, add Spicy Chicken Broth or water. To thicken, simmer 2 to 3 minutes longer or as needed for the desired consistency.

EASIER MOLE

Makes 4 cups (1 kg)

1 (8 ¼ ounces, or 233 g) jar of mole poblano (Doña Maria brand is very good.)

1 (3.1 ounces, or 87 g) Mexican chocolate tablet or 3 ounces (85 g) semisweet chocolate, broken into small pieces

4 cups (946 ml) Spicy Chicken Broth (page 74), or store-bought

5 teaspoons (27 g) peanut butter

2 teaspoons cinnamon

1 teaspoon ground cloves

1 teaspoon salt

1 teaspoon cayenne pepper

If you're not familiar with mole and want to get an idea what it tastes like before you commit to the Real Deal Mole recipe, give this one a try. And if you are already a mole fan but don't want to tackle the "scratch" version, give this very streamlined version a try. Start with a jar of mole paste, dilute and doctor it, cook through, and you've got a darn good mole.

1 In a blender jar or work bowl of a food processor, combine the mole, chocolate, and Spicy Chicken Broth. Use a wooden spoon to break up any pieces of mole paste.

2 Process for 2 to 3 minutes or until smooth. Add the peanut butter, cinnamon, ground cloves, salt, and cayenne. Process for 1 minute longer.

3 In a medium saucepan over medium heat, cook the processed sauce until it simmers. Reduce the heat and simmer for 10 minutes or until the sauce is the consistency of ketchup. To thin, add Spicy Chicken Broth or water. To thicken, simmer 2 to 3 minutes longer or as needed to reach the desired consistency.

WHO POPULARIZED THE TORTILLA CHIP?

Rebecca Webb Carranza was the owner of a Mexican delicatessen and tortilla factory in Los Angeles. She began selling fried remnants of discarded tortillas for a dime a bag.

SOUR CREAM ENCHILADA SAUCE

Makes 4 cups (1.1 kg)

¼ cup (55 g) butter or (60 ml) vegetable oil

¼ cup (31 g) all-purpose flour

2 cups (475 ml) Spicy Chicken Broth (page 74), or store-bought

1 cup (115 g) shredded Monterey Jack cheese

½ teaspoon salt

¼ teaspoon white pepper

1½ cups (345 g) sour cream, plus ½ cup (120 ml) Spicy Chicken Broth; or 2 cups (460 g) Mexican crema or 2 cups (448 g) crème fraîche

This sauce is the Tex-Mex equivalent of Alfredo sauce. Although most often used on chicken enchiladas, it could as easily be used on chicken fried steak, pasta, mashed white or sweet potatoes, or any dish complemented by a creamy white sauce.

It is also one of the few sauces in this chapter that doesn't reheat well. Because of the sour cream, the sauce will break or curdle when reheated. However, you can make this sauce in advance up to the point of adding sour cream. That said, I prefer the addition of milder, thinner Mexican crema. But either one will work. I used "sour cream" in the recipe title because that is the most familiar name for this type of sauce most often used on chicken enchiladas.

If you're wondering, *crema* is the Mexican version of crème fraîche. Both are milder than sour cream, neither as tangy nor as thick. That's why I prefer crema, but will use crème fraîche for this sauce if crema is not available. Mexican crema is available in Hispanic markets and in many Southwestern supermarkets with a strong Mexican customer base.

To make the sauce ahead, complete step 3 below and stop. The sauce may be refrigerated up to 2 days. Just before you are ready to assemble the enchiladas or to serve, reheat the base to the boiling point. Off the heat, add the sour cream or crema; keep warm. Use as called for in any enchilada or other tortilla recipe or as a sauce.

1 In a medium saucepan over medium heat, melt the butter or heat the oil until shimmery. Using a wooden spoon, stir in the flour and cook until well-blended and bubbly, stirring constantly.

2 Using a wire whisk, gradually stir in the Spicy Chicken Broth. Stirring constantly, cook until the mixture thickens and bubbles.

3 Remove from the heat and whisk in the cheese, salt, and pepper, stirring until smooth and all the cheese is melted.

4 If serving or using immediately, stir in the sour cream, additional Spicy Chicken Broth, Mexican crema, or crème fraîche. Do not allow the sauce to boil but keep warm.

5 To make ahead, stop after step 3. Allow the sauce to cool to room temperature in the pan. Transfer to a container with a lid and refrigerate for up to 2 days.

6 To finish the sauce after refrigerating the base, reheat gently to the boiling point. Remove from the heat and stir in the sour cream or Mexican crema. Do not allow the sauce to boil but keep warm.

QUESO (CHEESE SAUCE OR DIP)

Makes 3 cups (750 g)

8 ounces (225 g) Velveeta cheese, cut into several chunks for faster melting

1 cup (115 g) shredded cheddar or Pepper Jack cheese

1 cup (235 ml) Spicy Chicken Broth (page 74), additional as needed

¾ cup (120 g) coarsely chopped white or yellow onion

1 cup (144 g) coarsely chopped fresh mild green chile, such as New Mexico, Anaheim, or poblano chilli, seeded or ½ cup (72 g) chopped roasted New Mexico, Anaheim, or poblano chile (page 40)

½ cup (90 g) chopped tomato, rinsed and drained

Along with Tex-Mex Chili Gravy, this is a primal Tex-Mex sauce for enchiladas, burritos, or whatever you want it on. It is also a great dip for chips. Frankly, I can eat Queso as cheese soup, although this is something I do when no one is looking. Slurping Queso isn't pretty to watch.

If you're skeptical after looking at the ingredients, consider why you should use Velveeta: It melts without stringing and makes refrigeration and reheating easy. You can use traditional yellow Velveeta, or, if you can find it, Velveeta Queso Blanco. The white cheese version of Velveeta is available in many Hispanic grocery stores. To up the flavor ante, I added some shredded cheddar to this recipe.

Queso may be made using a double boiler, microwave, or slow cooker. Using a slow cooker takes a while, but it is fail-safe, and the Queso will stay warm for serving.

1 Fill the bottom of a double boiler with water to the fill line. Place over high heat and bring to a boil. Lower the heat to simmer.

2 In the top of the double boiler over the hot water, combine the cheeses and Spicy Chicken Broth. Cook, stirring every 3 to 4 minutes, for 10 minutes or until the cheeses are melted and blended with the liquid.

3 Add the onion, green chile, and tomato. Over very low heat, cook, stirring frequently, until the vegetables are tender, about 15 minutes.

4 Add more Spicy Chicken Broth to thin the sauce as desired. You will want it thicker for chips and thinner for an enchilada sauce.

5 Check the water in the bottom of the double boiler to make sure it does not boil away. Replenish as needed. Maintain a low simmer.

6 To reheat, microwave on 50 percent power, stirring frequently, for about 1 minute.

To make Queso in a microwave: Combine the cheeses and Spicy Chicken Broth in large microwave safe bowl. Microwave on high power for 60 seconds, stirring once. Continue to microwave for 30-second intervals, stirring each time, until the cheese is melted and blended. Set aside. In a 1-pint (475 ml) size microwave safe measuring cup, combine the onions, green chilli, and tomato with an additional ¼ cup (60 ml) of Spicy Chicken Broth. Microwave on high power, stirring every 30 seconds, for 2 to 3 minutes or until the vegetables are soft. Add to the melted cheese and heat through on medium power.

To make Queso in a slow cooker: Combine all the ingredients on low. Stir frequently, until well-blended and the vegetables are soft, at least 1 hour.

EBAR QUESO

Makes 3 cups (780g)

8 ounces (225 g) Velveeta cheese, cut into several chunks for faster melting

1 cup (115 g) shredded cheddar cheese

1 cup (235 ml) Spicy Chicken Broth (page 74), plus additional as needed

½ to ¾ cup (113 to 170 g) Chorizo (page 72), crumbled, fried, and drained; or ½ cup (110 g) Ground Beef Filling (page 60), well-drained of cooking liquid

½ cup (113 g) Guacamole (page 105)

¼ cup (60 g) sour cream or Mexican crema

Cayenne pepper, for garnish

This recipe is based on one of my favorite offerings at one of my favorite restaurants in the world. EBar Tex-Mex Grill is my Old East Dallas neighborhood hangout. This recipe, based on their special version of queso with some add-ins, is The Best. It's the ultimate queso for dipping chips. Blended, it makes a wonderful enchilada sauce. As with the basic queso it begins with, you can eat it like soup when no one's looking. Like basic Queso (page 99) it can be made in a double boiler, microwave, or slow cooker.

1 Fill the bottom of a double boiler with water to the fill line. Place over high heat and bring to a boil. Lower the heat to simmer.

2 In the top of the double boiler over the hot water, combine the cheeses and Spicy Chicken Broth. Cook, stirring every 3 to 4 minutes, for about 10 minutes, until the cheeses are melted and blended with the liquid.

3 Alternately, melt the cheese and stock in a microwave safe bowl on high power. Cook for 1 minute and stir. Repeat until the cheese is melted. Or, combine the stock and cheese in a slow cooker on high. Heat for 1 hour or until the cheese is melted. Blend the cheese and stock.

4 Add more Spicy Chicken Broth to thin the sauce as desired. You will want it thicker for chips and thinner for an enchilada sauce.

5 To serve, place the queso in a chafing dish over a low flame or serve in slow cooker on the lowest setting. Dollop mounds of Chorizo or Ground Beef Filling, guacamole, and sour cream on top. If using Mexican crema, drizzle it over the surface of the queso and dollops of stir-ins. Or, stir it all together for a really fabulous sauce.

Q: *Why should you always keep a good supply of cheese dip and tortilla chips?*

In queso-mergency.

RED SALSA

Makes about 3 cups (780 g)

3 cups (540 g) chopped fresh, ripe tomatoes or 2 cans (28 ounces, or 785 g each) chopped tomatoes, undrained

1 fresh serrano chile, stem removed, seeded and coarsely chopped

2 fresh jalapeños, stems removed, seeded and coarsely chopped

3 cloves of garlic

1 cup (160 g) chopped white or yellow onion

1¼ cups (285 ml) water

½ cup (8 g) chopped fresh cilantro leaves

1½ teaspoons salt

This is the basic salsa that scoops so well with tortilla chips. Piquant and flavorful, this salsa will store in your refrigerator for up to 2 weeks and goes great with just about any dish that uses tortillas or when used to perk up everything from scrambled eggs to baked potatoes.

While most of us are used to salsa served at room temperature, for a real treat, serve it warm with freshly fried, lightly salted chips. The flavor is soothing and mild at first taste and heats to a pleasing burn at the back of the mouth. It is always a good idea to wear food handler's gloves when working with fresh chiles.

One more thing, roasting fresh tomatoes and chiles gives a whole different taste: deeper, sweeter, and nuttier. Roasting also makes the chiles milder.

1 In a medium saucepan over high heat, combine the chopped tomatoes, chiles, garlic, onions, and water. Bring to a boil and then reduce the heat to very low and simmer for about 20 minutes or until all the ingredients are soft.

2 Allow to cool slightly.

3 In a blender jar or work bowl of a food processor, combine the cooked tomato mixture, cilantro, and salt. Process for about 1 minute or until smooth.

4 Serve warm or at room temperature.

Roasted Tomato Salsa: Preheat the broiler. Rinse and remove the cores from 2½ pounds [1.1 kg] of fresh chopped tomatoes. Remove the stems and seeds from the chiles. Place the tomatoes and chiles on a rimmed baking sheet or in a large heavy skillet. Place on a high rack under the broiler for 5 minutes or until the skin is puffed and browned or blackened, turning as needed. Do not peel. Allow to cool. Proceed with step 1 above, reducing the cooking time to 10 minutes.

GREEN TOMATILLO SALSA

Makes about 3 cups (780 g)

1 pound (455 g) fresh tomatillos, husked, rinsed and cut into quarters or 1 can (28 ounces, or 785 g) of tomatillos, undrained

1 jalapeño, stem and seeds removed

½ cup (8 g) cilantro leaves, loosely packed

¼ cup (40 g) coarsely chopped onion

1 teaspoon salt, or to taste

½ cup (120 ml) water, if using fresh tomatillos

This green salsa may be prepared using cooked or uncooked ingredients. It is crunchier and spicier when made with uncooked tomatillos. Using canned or roasted tomatillos makes for a milder salsa that can be stored longer in the refrigerator.

1 In a blender jar or work bowl of a food processor, combine the fresh tomatillos plus ½ cup (120 ml) of water or canned tomatillos and their liquid, jalapeño, cilantro leaves, chopped onion, and salt. Process by pulsing to evenly chop ingredients. The salsa should be somewhat chunky.

2 Adjust the seasoning to taste. Serve chilled or at room temperature.

3 It may be refrigerated for up to 2 days.

Roasted Tomatillo Salsa: Preheat the broiler. Remove the husks and rinse the tomatillos. Remove the stems and seeds from the jalapeño. Place the tomatillos and jalapeño on a rimmed baking sheet lined with foil or in a large heavy skillet. Place under the broiler until the skin is puffed and browned or blackened, turning as needed, for about 5 minutes. Allow to cool slightly. Combine the roasted tomatillos and jalapeños and any juices in the bottom of the roasting pan plus ½ cup (120 ml) of water in a blender jar or work bowl of a food processor. Proceed with step 1 above. It may be refrigerated for up to 1 week.

CHIPOTLE SALSA

Makes 3 cups (750 g)

1 to 3 chipotle peppers

3 cups (780 g) Red Salsa (page 101), Roasted Tomato Salsa (page 101), Green Tomatillo Salsa (page 102), or Roasted Tomatillo Salsa (page 102)

Chipotle peppers are dried and smoked jalapeños, widely available canned and packed in adobo sauce, a savory marinade. Chipotles are also available where there's a large selection of dried chillies. The addition of chipotle pepper (canned or dried) adds a hot smokey flavor to any salsa and redefines its character. The more you add, the hotter and smokier the salsa.

1   Remove the stems from the chipotles. In a small saucepan over high heat, combine the chipotles and enough wáter to cover. Bring to a boil, remove from heat, cover, and soak for 10 minutes or until soft. Drain.

2   If using canned chipotles, shake off any excess adobo sauce.

3   Add the drained or canned chipotles to the desired salsa in the blender stage of preparation.

PICO DE GALLO (FRESH TOMATO AND CHILE SALSA)

Makes 2 cups (500 g)

1½ cups (270 g) chopped fresh tomatoes, cored and unpeeled

½ cup (80 g) chopped white or yellow onion

1 jalapeño (2 inches, or 5 cm long), finely chopped (seeded for very mild salsa)

½ cup (8 g) fresh cilantro leaves, coarsely chopped

½ teaspoon salt

This salsa is uncooked, a style known as *pico de gallo*, which literally translates to "rooster's beak." Pico de gallo is a classic garnish for fajitas but also makes a great topping for guacamole or tacos. Wear plastic food handlers' gloves when working with fresh chiles to safeguard sensitive eyes, nose, and mouth areas. Tempting as it might be to use a food processor to chop the tomatoes and onion, chop by hand, or else the tomatoes and onions will be mushy. Keep the tomatoes and onions uniform in size.

1   Place the tomatoes in a strainer to drain any excess juices.

2   In a medium bowl, combine the drained tomatoes, onion, jalapeño, cilantro, and salt. Gently stir the ingredients to blend well.

3   Chill for about 30 minutes before serving.

FRUIT SALSA

Makes 4 cups (1,040 g)

4 cups (600 g) chopped fruit, such as seedless watermelon, mango, strawberries, peaches (fresh or roasted), or pineapple (fresh or roasted), or a combination

½ cup (80 g) finely chopped red onion

¼ cup (4 g) fresh cilantro leaves, coarsely chopped

2 serrano chiles or 1 jalapeño, stems and seeds removed, finely chopped

2 tablespoons (30 ml) lime juice plus 1 teaspoon grated lime peel or zest

½ teaspoon salt, or to taste

1 small avocado, peeled and coarsely chopped (optional)

Salsas made with fruit are a logical extension of fresh tomato salsa. After all, tomatoes are classified as fruit. This is a recipe template for using just about any juicy sweet fruit in salsa, especially for use with Baja Fish Tacos (page 132) and Tacos with pork (page 71) or just about any chicken dish. Yes, you may add some chopped avocado if you like.

1   In a large bowl, combine the onion, cilantro, chiles or jalapeño, lime juice, lime zest, and salt. Toss the ingredients to mix well.

2   Cover tightly with plastic wrap and refrigerate 20 to 30 minutes before serving.

3   It may be refrigerated overnight.

4   Add avocado just before serving.

GUACAMOLE

Makes 3 cups (675 g)

2 cups (292 g) chopped ripe avocado (about 3, peeled and seeded)

1 cup (180 g) finely chopped tomato, rinsed and drained (optional)

½ cup (80 g) finely chopped white, yellow or red onion (optional)

¼ cup (4 g) finely chopped cilantro leaves (optional)

1 teaspoon (15 ml) lime juice, or to taste

1 teaspoon salt

When it comes to guacamole, less is more. A beautifully ripe avocado needs little embellishment: Some chopped tomato for color plus salt and a squeeze of lime juice may be close to perfect. If you want more add-ins, consider some chopped onion and cilantro.

1   In a medium bowl, use a potato masher or fork to mash the avocados to the desired consistency. Guacamole may be chunky or smooth.

2   If using stir in the drained tomatoes plus the onions and cilantro. Mix well.

3   Add the salt and lime juice. Adjust the seasoning to taste.

AVOCADO CREMA

Makes 3 cups (690 g)

1 pound (455 g) fresh tomatillos, husked and rinsed, or 1 can (28 ounces, or 785 g) of tomatillos, undrained

1 cup (235 ml) water, if using fresh tomatillos

2 serrano chiles, stems and seeds removed

2 cloves of garlic

4 sprigs of cilantro

1 teaspoon salt, or to taste

3 medium ripe avocados, peeled and seeded

¾ to 1 cup (180 to 230 g) Mexican crema or (168 to 224 g) crème fraîche

This is another of those sauces that can be a dip or a table sauce. Smooth and creamy with a titillating bite, the taste is a delicate balance of contrasting yums. The acid comes from tomatillos, the heat from serranos, and the tang from Mexican crema. Use crème fraîche if you can't find crema.

1 If using fresh tomatillos, cut them in half. In a medium saucepan over medium heat, combine the fresh tomatillos and water.

2 If using canned tomatillos, add the tomatillos and their liquid to a medium saucepan over medium heat.

3 Add the serranos and garlic to the tomatillos. Bring to a boil, reduce the heat, and simmer for 10 to 15 minutes until the ingredients are soft. Remove from the heat and let cool slightly.

4 In a blender jar or work bowl of food processor, combine the tomatillo mixture, cilantro, salt and avocados. Process until smooth, about 2 to 3 minutes.

5 Transfer the avocado mixture to a medium bowl. Blend in the crema or crème fraîche. Adjust the salt to taste.

6 Serve slightly chilled, at room temperature, or gently warmed but not hot.

What a Friend We Have in Cheeses

Tortillas and cheese go together like bread and butter. Whether cheese is sprinkled on, stuffed inside, melted, or used in a sauce, both corn and flour tortillas have a natural partner in cheese. Here's a list of the cheeses and their uses as called for in recipes throughout the book.

YELLOW CHEESES

Yellow cheese is the signature of Tex-Mex.

Cheddar

Cheddar is the most widely purchased and eaten cheese in the world. White cheddar is much less common than the typical yellow orange style. Made from cow's milk, cheddar is firm and melts easily, though it tends to string and clump. It is used in all types of tortilla dishes.

Colby

This is an orange-yellow like cheddar but milder and creamier and not as assertive in flavor. It is made from cow's milk. It melts well and is less likely to string or clump. Use it in any dish that calls for cheddar.

Colby Jack

This cheese is a yellow-and-white blend of Colby and Monterey Jack cheeses. It melts exceptionally well and is often used in Tex-Mex. Use it in any dish that calls for cheddar or Monterey Jack.

Longhorn

Yellow-orange in color, this cow's milk cheese is a form of Colby with similar properties.

Velveeta

This is the brand name of a mild-flavored yellow-orange processed cheese that melts and reheats well. It is both beloved by many and scorned by many, but it is very functional. Velveeta also produces a white cheese called *queso blanco*.

WHITE CHEESES

In general, white cheeses are more commonly used in Mexico and California.

Cotija

Closely resembling dry Parmesan, this cheese is salty and granular in texture when crumbled or ground. It is usually sprinkled on enchiladas, gorditas, sopes, and Mexican street tacos.

Monterey Jack

Similar in taste and texture to Colby, this cow's milk cheese is very mild. It melts exceptionally well and is widely used in Tex-Mex dishes with cheese.

Pepper Jack

This is Monterey Jack flavored with specks of red pepper flakes or jalapeños. It has a sharp pepper bite and melts well. Use it when you want a cheese with kick.

Queso Fresco

This means "fresh cheese." Crumbly and salty Mexican cheese, similar to feta though milder, it is used on refried beans or enchiladas. It melts well. Use it when you want a cheese with tang.

6

SNACKS AND STARTERS: TORTILLA CHIPS, NACHOS, CRISPS, QUESADILLAS, FLAUTAS, AND SOPES

Tortillas are an amazing medium for delivering food from hand to mouth—foods such as snacks and starters, especially when they're crisp. Fried tortillas in the form of chips are the perfect platform for beans and cheese and more elaborate toppings. They're the ultimate scoops for salsas and dips. They're also the base for nachos, a bar food and television-watching staple.

Flour tortillas get cheese toppings that transforms them into crisps and quesadillas. And then there's lesser known but oh-so-delicious sopes, three-bite platforms of corn flour—sort of a mini-pizza.

FRIED TORTILLA CHIPS

Makes 4 servings

8 Corn Tortillas (page 38) or Basic Flour Tortillas (page 50), or store-bought

Vegetable oil, for frying

Fine kosher or sea salt

Chips can be fresh fried using corn or flour tortillas. Either will work as dippers or for nachos, although corn chips are the more common choice.

1 Line a rimmed baking sheet with a double thickness of paper towels. Preheat the oven to 200ºF (93ºC).

2 In a deep fryer or electric skillet, heat at least 2 inches (5 cm) of oil to 350ºF (180ºC). Or use a deep skillet or other large pot and a candy/frying thermometer.

3 While the oil heats, stack the tortillas 3 or 4 at a time. Using a sharp knife, cut them in half. Then, cut each half into three triangles. Repeat until all the tortillas are cut.

4 Carefully add 4 tortilla triangles at a time to the hot oil. Using a wire skimmer or slotted spoon, stir the tortillas to prevent them from sticking together. Keep them submerged until golden brown, about 3 minutes.

5 Using a skimmer or a slotted spoon, remove the tortilla chips from the hot oil, allowing most of the oil to drain back into the pot.

6 Spread the chips in a single layer on paper towels to drain. Sprinkle with salt. Repeat with the remaining tortillas.

7 If cooking a large number of chips, separate the layers with additional paper towels.

8 Keep warm in a low oven or serve at room temperature.

Use: As chips with Red (page 101) or Green (page 102) Salsa; Queso (page 99), Guacamole (page 105); for Loaded Nachos (page 112).

NATIONAL TORTILLA CHIP DAY

It's a real thing: It happens annually on February 24th.

NACHO'S NACHOS

Makes 4 servings

4 Corn Tortillas (6 inches, or 15 cm) (page 38) or store-bought

Vegetable oil, for frying

1 cup (120 g) grated cheddar cheese

½ cup (52 g) drained pickled jalapeño slices

This is likely the way the original nachos were made by Igancio "Nacho" Anaya, maître d' at a club in Piedras Negras, Mexico, across the Rio Grande from Eagle Pass, Texas, in the early 40s when he improvised this snack. This recipe easily doubles for more servings or more nachos per person.

1   Preheat the oven to 425°F(220ºF, or gas mark 7).

2   In a skillet over medium-high heat, add ¼ inch (6 mm) of oil. Heat until the oil shimmers. Fry each tortilla in the hot oil for 2 to 3 minutes, turning once, until just crispy. Drain on paper towels.

3   On a rimmed baking sheet, arrange the tortillas in a single layer.

4   Sprinkle surface of each tortilla evenly with grated cheese. Top with the jalapeño slices.

5   Bake for 4 to 6 minutes until the cheese melts.

6   Before serving, cut each tortilla into four wedges using a sharp knife, pizza wheel, or kitchen scissors.

BALLPARKING NACHOS

Every Major League Baseball and National Football League stadium offers nachos. Only popcorn and soft drinks outsell nachos. You're outta there, hotdogs and Cracker Jack.

LOADED NACHOS

Makes 4 servings

4 cups (224 g) Fried Tortilla Chips (page 110) or store-bought

2 cups (344 g) Refried Beans (page 83)

2 cups (450 g) heated filling, such as Ground Beef (page 68), Shredded Beef Brisket (page 69), Fajitas, Beef, or Chicken (page 70), Shredded Braised Pork (page 71), Carnitas (page 71), Shredded Spicy Chicken (page 74), Shredded Roast Duck (page 75)

2 cups (240 g) grated cheddar, Colby, Colby Jack, Longhorn, Monterey Jack, Pepper Jack, or (300 g) queso fresco (see What a Friend We Have in Cheeses, page 107)

1 cup (104 g) drained pickled jalapeño slices

1 cup (225 g) Guacamole (page 105)

1 cup (180 g) chopped tomatoes, drained and rinsed

1 cup (230 g) sour cream or ½ cup (115 g) Mexican crema

Nacho's Nachos are the primeval nacho. This version is the more familiar everything-but-the-kitchen-sink rendition found in sports bars, as well as in some Mexican restaurants. Using fresh fried corn tortilla chips makes for even better nachos, but I get it if you'd rather make life simpler and buy restaurant-style corn tortilla chips. White or yellow corn, it's your choice.

The list of fillings provides lots of options if you want a protein layer. Use whatever you choose or nothing at all. Ditto for the after-oven toppings, starting with the Guacamole in step 7.

1 Preheat the oven to 425ºF (220ºC, or gas mark 7).

2 Using a rubber spatula or wooden spoon, lightly spread each chip with a thin layer of refried beans.

3 In a rimmed baking pan or other shallow ovenproof baking dish, arrange the tortillas in a single layer, with the edges slightly overlapping.

4 Dollop even amounts of filling on top of each chip.

5 Sprinkle the surface of each tortilla evenly with grated cheese. Top with the jalapeño slices.

6 Bake for 4 to 6 minutes until the cheese melts.

7 Remove from the oven and place dollops of Guacamole evenly around the melted cheese layer.

8 Sprinkle the surface evenly with pieces of tomato.

9 Dollop small mounds of sour cream evenly around the pan of nachos or drizzle Mexican crema over the nachos. Serve immediately.

Q:
What do you call chips that aren't yours?
Nachos, sucka!

ARIZONA CHEESE CRISPS

Makes 4 servings

4 Basic Flour Tortillas (page 50), large size, as for burritos, or use store-bought

4 teaspoons (19 g) butter, softened or melted

2 cups (240 g) grated cheese, such as cheddar, Colby, Colby Jack, Longhorn, Monterey Jack, Pepper Jack, or (300 g) queso fresco (see What a Friend We Have in Cheeses, page 107)

½ cup (72 g) chopped roasted green chillies (page 40) or (50 g) chopped green onions

This is the signature tortilla snack of Arizona, particularly Tucson. Made from flour tortillas, Arizona Cheese Crisps are the stripped down love child of a chalupa and a quesadilla. Open-faced like a chalupa, but made with a flour tortilla, the Arizona Cheese Crisp is crunchier than a quesadilla but without a top crust tortilla or elaborate toppings.

If you make your own tortillas for this recipe, press as thin as possible and as large in diameter as possible—burrito-size but thinner.

1 Preheat the oven to 350ºF (180ºC, or gas mark 4).

2 Using a rubber spatula or brush, evenly coat one side of each tortilla with butter all the way to the edges. Arrange the buttered tortillas in a single layer on a baking sheet.

3 Place the tortillas in the oven and bake for 10 minutes or until lightly toasted and crisp.

4 Remove from the oven and evenly sprinkle the surface of each tortilla with grated cheese.

5 Evenly sprinkle green chillies or green onions over the cheese. Onions also may be reserved as a garnish after baking, if uncooked onions are preferred.

6 Place the tortillas in the oven and bake for 5 minutes or until the cheese is melted and bubbly. Serve immediately.

Q: *What do you call a tough tortilla chip?*
Macho nacho.

FLAUTAS (TAQUITOS)

Makes 4 servings

12 Corn or Basic Flour Tortillas (page 38 and 50 or store-bought

Vegetable oil, for frying

2 cups (450 g) or a combination of heated fillings, such as:
• Ground Beef (page 68)
• Shredded Beef Brisket (page 69)
• Fajitas, Beef or Chicken (page 70)
• Shredded Braised Pork (page 71)
• Carnitas (page 71)
• Shredded Spicy Chicken (page 74)
• Shredded Roast or Hot-Smoked Duck (page 75)
• Shrimp or Crab (page 76)
• Fried Shrimp (page 76)
• Beer Batter Fried Fish (page 78)
• Grilled or Broiled Fish (page 77)
• Pinto Beans (page 80)
• Black Beans (page 81)
• Refried Pinto or Black Beans (page 83)

1 cup (120 g) grated cheddar, Colby, Colby Jack, Longhorn, Monterey Jack, or Pepper Jack (see What a Friend We Have in Cheeses, (page 107) (optional)

Queso (page 99)

Red Salsa (page 101)

Green Tomatillo Salsa (page 102)

Guacamole (page 105)

Sometimes called *taquitos*, these fried tortilla rods are named for "flutes" because of their long, skinny appearance. The idea is the same basic formula as for filling an enchilada except that, once filled and rolled tight, a flauta is fried crisp for eating out of hand. A variety of dipping sauces, including salsa, queso, and guacamole, make flautas great for sharing.

Traditionally, flautas are made with corn tortillas, but flour tortillas also work.

1 In a deep fryer or electric skillet, heat at least 2 inches (5 cm) of oil to 375ºF (190ºC). Or use a deep skillet or other large pot and a candy/frying thermometer.

2 Spread about 2 tablespoons (28 g) of filling or 1 tablespoon (15 g) of filling plus 1 table-spoon (8 g) of cheese in a line the width of a tortilla.

3 Tightly roll the tortilla around the filling into a cylinder. Secure the ends with one or two toothpicks. Repeat with the remaining tortillas.

4 When the oil is hot, carefully lower the rolled tortillas into the hot oil. Fry no more than 4 at a time for 2 to 3 minutes, or until golden brown.

5 Drain on paper towels.

6 Discard the toothpicks and serve with the desired dipping sauces.

Q:
What do you call a dangerous flauta?

Gangster wrap.

CHALUPAS

Makes 4 servings

8 Corn Tortillas (page 38) or Basic Flour Tortillas (page 50), or use store-bought

Vegetable oil, for frying

2 cups (450 g) or a combination of heated fillings, such as:
• Ground Beef (page 68)
• Shredded Beef Brisket (page 69)
• Fajitas, Beef or Chicken (page 70)
• Shredded Braised Pork (page 71)
• Carnitas (page 71)
• Shredded Spicy Chicken (page 74)
• Shredded Roast Duck (page 75)
• Pinto Beans (page 80)
• Black Beans (page 81)
• Refried Beans (page 83)

2 cups (144 g) shredded iceberg lettuce

1 cup (250 g) Pico de Gallo (page 104) or chopped fresh tomatoes, rinsed and drained

2 cups (240 g) grated cheddar, Colby, Colby Jack, Longhorn, Monterey Jack, Pepper Jack, or (300 g) queso fresco, or ½ cup (40 g) cotija (see What a Friend We Have in Cheeses, (page 107)

Salsa(s) of choice (page 101 to 104)

The Tex-Mex–style chalupas I'm most familiar with are built on flat, crisp-fried corn tortillas. But the Spanish word means "little boat," evoking the shape of snacks called chalupas built on crisp-fried tortillas with raised edges, sort of like a canoe. Flat or with raised edges, the shape functions as a saucer or shallow bowl.

As with many tortilla dishes, both corn and flour tortillas are used for chalupas. And the fillings are as varied as those for tacos. In fact, a chalupa is a flat or open-faced crispy taco. It is easier to fry the tortillas flat than to shape them but suit yourself.

If you opt to shape the tortillas, have ready a set of tongs as well as a skimmer or slotted spoon to hold the tortilla in the shape you desire while it sets in the hot oil.

1 Line a rimmed baking sheet with a double thickness of paper towels. Preheat the oven to 200ºF (90ºC).

2 In a deep fryer or electric skillet, heat at least 2 inches (5 cm) of oil to 350ºF (180ºC). Or use a deep skillet or other large pot and a candy/frying thermometer.

3 While the oil heats, ready all the ingredients for filling the chalupa. Arrange in an assembly line. Keep heated fillings warm.

4 Fry the tortillas one at a time.

5 For flat chalupas, carefully slide tortilla into hot oil. It should float and bubble. Fry for about 30 seconds. Using tongs, turn and fry until golden brown and crisp.

6 For "little boats," carefully slide tortilla into hot oil. It should float and bubble. Fry for about 30 seconds. Using tongs, fold edges of tortilla up, using a skimmer to help hold the shape until the dough fries crisp, another 30 to 45 seconds. Turn to brown and crisp on all sides.

7 Remove to paper towel-lined pan to drain. Keep warm in the oven. Repeat with the remaining tortillas.

8 To fill the chalupas, spread ¼ cup (55 g) of filling on or in a chalupa shell. Add 2 tablespoons (9 g) of shredded lettuce and 1 tablespoon (76 g) of Pico de Gallo or chopped tomato. Top with 1 tablespoon (8 g) of grated cheese or a sprinkle of cotija.

9 If making ahead for each diner to garnish, add the filling and keep the chalupas warm in the oven until ready to serve.

Q: *Why can't you trust a chalupa?*
It always spills the beans.

QUESADILLAS

Makes 4 servings

8 Basic Flour Tortillas
(page 50), or store-bought

Vegetable oil or
cooking spray

3 cups (360 g) grated
cheddar, Colby, Colby Jack,
Longhorn, Monterey Jack,
Pepper Jack, or (450 g)
queso fresco (see What
a Friend We Have in
Cheeses, page 107)

1 cup (225 g) or a
combination of heated
fillings, such as:
Ground Beef (page 68),
• Shredded Beef Brisket
  (page 69)
• Fajitas, Beef or Chicken
  (page 70)
• Shredded Braised Pork
  (page 71)
• Carnitas (page 71)
• Shredded Spicy Chicken
  (page 74)
• Shredded Roast Duck
  (page 75)
• Pinto Beans (page 80)
• Black Beans (page 81)
• Roasted chillies cut into
  strips (page 40)
• Grilled onions and pep-
  pers (page 87)

Salsa(s) of choice
(page 101 to 104)

Guacamole (page 105)

These are the double crusts pizzas or calzones of Mexican food. Made with flour tortillas, quesadillas sandwich a melted layer of cheese, as well as other fillings of choice. Quesadillas can be made by placing a top crust tortilla over the cheese layer or by folding the tortilla like a taco or calzone. Griddled till the cheese melts and the outside is toasted, quesadillas are great for kids of all ages who adore grilled cheese sandwiches. In its simplest form, this is a Southwestern grilled cheese sandwich.

1   Preheat the oven to 200ºF (90ºC). Have ready a baking sheet.

2   Heat a large heavy bottom skillet (I prefer well-seasoned cast iron), griddle with non-stick surface, or comal over medium heat to 350ºF (180ºC) or until water sprinkled on the surface "dances" and quickly evaporates.

3   Using a paper towel, carefully rub a thin layer of oil in the bottom of the pan or spray with cooking oil spray.

4   Place a flour tortilla in the pan. Using tongs, move the tortilla around to soak up a bit of the oil so it doesn't stick.

FOR STACKED QUESADILLAS

1   Arrange ⅓ cup (40 g) of cheese in an even layer on top of the tortilla in the pan. Dot the surface of the cheese with 1 to 2 tablespoons (15 to 28 g) of other filling(s) as desired. Sprinkle a bit more cheese over the filling. Top with a second tortilla. Brush lightly with oil. Cook for 1 minute or until the bottom begins to brown.

2   Using a spatula, quickly flip the quesadilla. Cook for 1 minute longer or until the bottom of the tortilla begins to brown. Using a spatula, remove it from the pan. Slice and serve immediately. Or keep warm while making quesadillas with the remaining ingredients.

FOR FOLDED QUESADILLAS

1   Arrange 3 tablespoons (23 g) of cheese evenly on half the tortilla in the pan. Dot the surface of the cheese with 1 tablespoon (15 g) of other filling(s) as desired. Sprinkle 2 more tablespoons (30 g) of cheese over the filling.

2   Using a spatula or tongs, fold the tortilla in half. Use a spatula or tongs to press the edges together. Cook for 1 minute or until the bottom begins to brown. Using a spatula, quickly flip the quesadilla. Cook 30 seconds longer to brown the other side. Using a spatula, remove it from the pan. Slice and serve immediately. Or keep warm while making quesadillas with the remaining ingredients.

3   Serve the quesadillas with Salsa and Guacamole, as desired. Dip into salsa or spread guacamole on top.

MEXICAN STREET SOPES

Makes 4 servings

1½ cups (338 g) heated fillings, such as Shredded Beef Brisket (page 69), Shredded Braised Pork (page 71), Carnitas (page 71), Shredded Spicy Chicken (page 74), Shredded Roast Duck (page 75)

½ cup (80 g) finely chopped white onion

⅓ cup (39 g) very thinly sliced or julienned radishes

1 avocado, peeled, seeded, and chopped

½ cup (90 g) chopped tomato, rinsed and drained, or (125 g) Pico de Gallo (page 104)

½ cup (52 g) sliced pickled jalapeños

½ cup (8 g) finely chopped cilantro leaves

¾ cup (60 g) cotija (see What a Friend We Have In Cheeses, page 107)

Salsa of choice (page 101-104)

12 fresh fried Sopes (page 48)

Sopes aren't true tortillas, at least as most of us think of tortillas. Made of masa, sopes are more like corn flour tart shells, 3 inches (7.5 cm) in diameter with slightly raised sides to hold the filling. If preparing sopes, ready all the fillings and garnishes so hot sopes can be filled and eaten immediately.

Sopes are more authentically Mexican than many tortilla dishes that have been Americanized. If you've never had sopes, you will quickly become a serious fan. In Mexico, shredded beef or chicken are the traditional fillings.

The more flavors to pile onto the fillings the better, but don't let this extensive list intimidate you. For the sake of authenticity, at least top the filling with white onion, cilantro, and cotija. Serve with salsa.

1 Before making the sopes, ready all the ingredients for filling the sopes. Arrange in an assembly line, keep heated fillings warm.

2 Prepare the sopes (page 47).

3 Fill each sope with 2 tablespoons (28 g) of heated filling.

4 Top with a sprinkling of desired garnishes: white onion, radishes, avocado, tomato or Pico de Gallo, pickled jalapeños, cilantro, and cotija.

5 Serve with your salsa of choice.

7

TACOS, MORE TACOS, AND BREAKFAST TACOS, PLUS BURRITOS, CHIMICHANGAS, AND GORDITAS

No tortilla dish has been embraced and adapted more than the taco. It's amazing since the tortilla is thousands of years old yet the history of the taco as we know it likely dates to 18th century silver mines in Mexico.

That's the conclusion of taco researcher Jeffrey M. Pilcher of the University of Minnesota. The history professor has spent a quarter of a century chronicling the history, politics, and evolution of Mexican food and the cultural arc of tacos in the U.S. That work produced Pilcher's 2012 book *Planet Taco: A Global History of Mexican Food.*

Tacos were a handy lunch for silver miners, believes Pilcher. His work documents the immigration of the taco to the American Southwest, where Mexican-Americans reinvented them and Southern California businessman Glen Bell mass-marketed tacos to Anglo palates with the Taco Bell crunchy shell. Bell developed a fryer to quickly produce crispy taco shells (although his machine was not the first) and started selling crispy tacos from his hamburger stand in 1951. He launched Taco Bell in 1962, and sixteen years later, he sold what had become a national chain with hundreds of franchisees to PepsiCo.

That's how the crispy corn taco became the mass image of the taco until the soft taco, street taco, and breakfast taco awakening that dawned about thirty years ago.

In this book, we will make them all and explore the joys of Mexican Breakfast—a totally tortilla-centric meal.

CRISPY TACOS

Makes 4 servings

Vegetable oil, for frying

12 Corn or Basic Flour Tortillas (page 38 and 50), or store-bought

2 cups (450 g) or a combination of heated fillings, such as:
Ground Beef (page 68)
- Shredded Beef Brisket (page 69)
- Fajitas, Beef or Chicken (page 70)
- Shredded Braised Pork (page 71)
- Carnitas (page 71)
- Shredded Spicy Chicken (page 74)
- Shredded Roast or Hot-Smoked Duck (page 75)
- Shrimp or Crab (page 76)
- Fried Shrimp (page 76), Beer Batter Fried Fish (page 78)
- Grilled or Broiled Fish (page 77)
- Pinto Beans (page 80)
- Black Beans (page 81)
- Refried Pinto or Black Beans (page 83)

2 cups (144 g) shredded iceberg lettuce

1 cup (250 g) Pico de Gallo (page 104), or 1 cup (180 g) chopped tomato, rinsed and drained

1 cup (120 g) grated cheddar, Colby, Colby Jack, Longhorn, Monterey Jack, or Pepper Jack (see What a Friend We Have in Cheeses, page 107)

A fast food crispy corn taco used to be the first taco experience for a lot of folks who weren't of Hispanic heritage or didn't live in the Southwest. That's the Taco Bell model that led the way to packages of readymade (usually stale-tasting) shells on supermarket shelves. If that's still your taco shell baseline, you may not be a fan of crispy tacos. But fresh-fried corn or flour tortillas for taco shells can alter your taco reality.

By fresh-frying tortillas, you can determine how crispy you want them. For softer taco shells with a bit of outside crunch, fry just until they hold a fold. For crisp, molded shells that crack like chips, let 'em go a little longer, all the way to light brown.

There are all sorts of racks for shaping and frying tortillas for tacos. There are also racks for draining taco shells after frying and to hold them upright for easier stuffing. Most of these work great. They are helpful but not necessary. A pair of tongs and a skimmer or slotted spoon will work just fine.

Unless you are obsessed with homemade tortillas (it's okay if you are), feel free to use store-bought tortillas, especially if you will fry them super crisp.

1 Preheat the oven to 200°F (90°C) and line a rimmed baking sheet with a double layer of paper towels.

2 In a deep fryer or electric skillet, heat at least 2 inches (5 cm) of oil to 365°F (185°C). Or use a deep skillet or other large pot and a candy/frying thermometer.

3 While the oil heats, ready all the ingredients for filling the tacos. Arrange in an assembly line. Keep heated fillings warm.

4 To fry the taco shells, carefully slide 1 tortilla into the hot oil. It should float and bubble. Fry for about 15 seconds. Using tongs, turn and fold over. Fry for another 15 to 30 seconds until golden brown and crisp. Do not let the folded edges touch or they could seal. Leave some space between the edges for stuffing.

5 Use a skimmer or slotted spoon to remove the taco shell from the oil, allowing exceess to drain back into the pot. Place the taco shell directly on paper towels to drain or in a rack over paper towels. Repeat with the remaining tortillas. Keep warm in the oven.

6 Fill each taco shell with 2 tablespoons (28 g) of heated filling. Add 2 tablespoons (9 g) of shredded lettuce and 1 tablespoon (16 g) of Pico de Gallo or chopped tomato. Top with 1 tablespoon (8 g) of grated cheese.

7 If making ahead for each diner to garnish, add the filling and keep the tacos warm in the oven until ready to serve.

Q: *How do tacos say grace?*
Lettuce pray.

PUFFY TACOS

Makes 4 servings

2 cups (450 g) or a combination of heated fillings, such as:
- Ground Beef (page 68)
- Shredded Beef Brisket (page 69)
- Fajitas, Beef or Chicken (page 70)
- Shredded Braised Pork (page 71)
- Carnitas (page 71)
- Shredded Spicy Chicken (page 74)
- Shredded Roast or Hot-Smoked Duck (page 75)
- Shrimp or Crab (page 76)
- Fried Shrimp (page 76)
- Beer Batter Fried Fish (page 78)
- Grilled or Broiled Fish (page 77)
- Pinto Beans (page 80)
- Black Beans (page 81)
- Refried Pinto or Black Beans (page 83)

2 cups (144 g) shredded iceberg lettuce

1 cup (250 g) Pico de Gallo (page 104), or 1 cup (180 g) chopped tomato, rinsed and drained

1 cup (120 g) grated cheddar, Colby, Colby Jack, Longhorn, Monterey Jack (see What a Friend We Have in Cheeses, page 107)

Masa (page 12) or fresh masa (page 42) for Corn Tortillas (page 38) or dough for Basic Flour Tortillas (page 50)

Vegetable oil, for frying

These treats are traced to San Antonio where brothers Henry and Ray Lopez came up with the concept at Ray's Drive-In in the 50s. As often happens in the food business, grease is thicker than blood, and the brothers split a number of years later. Henry opened his own namesake restaurant, Henry's Puffy Tacos, in 1978 and had the good sense to name it after the signature dish.

A puffy taco starts just like a corn tortilla, with masa and a tortilla press. From there, the just-pressed tortilla goes into a bubbling cauldron of hot fat instead of on to a hot comal. The result is a puffy taco shell, crispy on the outside, soft and chewy on the inside.

The original style comes out of the fryer with a puffy, u-shaped crust. It resembles a folded taco. There's another style of puffy "taco," although it is more like a chalupa in that the tortilla is flat with a puffy dome. Crack the dome, and the filling goes inside.

Although puffy tacos are traditionally made with corn masa, flour tortilla dough also works. Flour tortillas puff more, but the taste of corn tortillas is incomparable.

1 Before making the puffy taco shells, ready all the ingredients for filling the tacos. Arrange in an assembly line. Keep heated fillings warm.

2 Make the masa or dough according to the recipe (page 38 and 50).

3 In a deep fryer or electric skillet, heat at least 2 inches (5 cm) of oil to 375ºF (190ºC). Or use a deep skillet or other large pot and a candy/frying thermometer.

- Form the masa or dough balls and press according to the recipe.
- For puffy corn tortillas, shape, press, and fry the tortillas one at a time.
- For puffy flour tortillas, shape and press tortillas and *then* fry one at a time.

continued

TIPS FOR SUCCESSFUL PUFFY TACO SHELLS

1 Masa from fresh or homemade nixtamal, page 42, makes the puffiest taco shells.

2 Masa made with masa harina should be a bit wetter for puffy tacos than for regular corn tortillas.

3 If not using an appliance with a thermostat to maintain temperature, use a candy/fry thermometer to keep oil at a steady 375ºF (190ºC). If the temperature goes below, the taco shells will be greasy. If the temperature gets too high, the tortillas will burn, and there is risk of fire.

4 Be prepared to work fast. Better yet, work in pairs. This goes smoother if one person shapes tortillas while the other does the frying.

continued

4 To fry the tortillas, using a slotted metal spatula, carefully slide the tortilla into the hot oil. While frying, use a long-handled metal spoon to baste the tortilla with the hot oil. This will cause the tortilla to puff.

5 After about 1 minute of frying and basting, use the spatula to flip the tortilla. Quickly press the spoon into the middle of the tortilla to form a taco shape. Fry for 1 minute longer or until the tortilla is golden and holds its shape.

6 Using a spatula, remove from the oil, allowing any excess to drip back into the pan. Drain on paper towels. Repeat with the remaining tortillas.

7 Crack the dome of each puffy taco and fill with 2 tablespoons (28 g) of heated filling. Add 2 tablespoons (9 g) of shredded lettuce and 1 tablespoon (16 g) of Pico de Gallo or chopped tomato. Top with 1 tablespoon (8 g) of grated cheese. Serve immediately.

EASY PUFFY FLOUR TORTILLA "TACO" SHELLS

Sadly, store-bought prepared corn tortillas won't puff, but store-bought prepared flour tortillas will. In a deep fryer, electric skillet, or heavy skillet over medium-high heat, heat at least 2 inches (5 cm) of vegetable oil to 375°F (190°C). Using a slotted metal spatula, carefully slide a store-bought flour tortilla into the hot oil. Cook on 1 side for 2 minutes or until the tortilla puffs and creates a golden, crispy dome. While frying, use a long-handled metal spoon to baste the tortilla with hot oil. This is what causes the dome to puff. Using tongs or a skimmer, remove the tortilla to paper towels to drain. Crack the dome and fill.

Q:
How many guys does it take to eat the world's largest taco?

Just Juan.

Mexican Street Tacos

Tacos sold by Mexican street vendors, an open-faced style widely adopted by taco and Mexican food trucks, are the textural and flavor antithesis of the generic American fast food crispy taco. This style double-layers (stacks) two soft, mini-corn tortillas for filling. In Mexico, the filling is usually pork or chicken, although you may select any filling that you like, from beef to fish. (See Chapter 5, Fillings, page 67.)

Mexican street-style toppings also vary from those typical of American-style tacos. The accoutrements usually include finely chopped white onion, fresh chillies, and cilantro. Red or green salsa is the typical sauce. Notice: there's no grated cheddar or Monterey jack cheese. White, dry Mexican-style cheeses such as cotija, a crumbly cow's milk cheese, are the quesos of choice.

MEXICAN STREET TACOS

Makes 4 servings (8 regular size or 12 mini corn tacos)

8 Corn Tortillas (6 or 7 inches, or 15 to 18 cm) or 24 mini Corn Tortillas (3 or 4 inches, or 7.5 to 10 cm) (page 38), or store-bought

2 cups (450 g) or a combination of heated fillings, such as:
• Ground Beef (page 68)
• Shredded Beef Brisket (page 69)
• Fajitas, Beef or Chicken (page 70)
• Shredded Braised Pork (page 71)

• Carnitas (page 71)
• Shredded Spicy Chicken (page 74)
• Shredded Roast Duck (page 75)

1 cup (16 g) finely chopped fresh cilantro

1 cup (160 g) finely chopped white onion

½ cup (72 g) finely chopped fresh serrano chile

½ cup (40 g) cotija cheese

8 to 12 small lime wedges

If you are making your own corn tortillas for Mexican street tacos and want to be authentic, make them smaller. Instead of 6 or 7 inches (15 or 18 cm) in diameter, try for 3 or 4 inches (7.5 or 10 cm).

1 Ready all the ingredients for filling the tacos. Arrange in an assembly line. Keep heated fillings warm.

2 Press or shape and bake fresh Corn Tortillas (page 26 and 29). Keep warm (page 33).

3 If using store-bought tortillas, heat a comal or heavy skillet until water sprinkled on the surface dances and quickly evaporates. If desired, spray with cooking oil spray or apply a very light layer of oil. Heat the tortillas and keep warm (page 33).

4 If using small tacos, use two tortillas. Stack one on top of another, fill, and serve open-faced. Fill a large tortilla with 2 tablespoons (28 g) of filling; use 1 tablespoon (15 g) of filling for small ones. Serve the large tacos folded or open-faced for easier garnishing.

5 Garnish as desired with 1 teaspoon of cilantro, 1 teaspoon of white onion, ¼ teaspoon of fresh chile or to taste, 1 teaspoon of cotija, and a lime wedge for squeezing over fillings just before eating.

Q: *Wife to husband: Why do you eat a taco using a tortilla for a napkin?*
Husband: Because when stuff falls out, I've already got another taco.

BAJA FISH TACOS

Makes 4 servings

12 Corn or Basic Flour Tortillas (page 38 and 50), or store-bought

2 cups (450 g) or a combination of heated fillings, such as Shrimp or Crab (page 76), Fried Shrimp (page 76), Beer Batter Fried Fish (page 78), Grilled or Broiled Fish (page 77)

2 cups (200 g) Creamy, Spicy, Maybe Sweet Slaw (page 88)

1 cup (250 g) Pico de Gallo (page 104), or 1 cup (180 g) chopped tomato, rinsed and drained

1 cup (230 g) Mexican crema or (224 g) crème fraîche

This is the style of taco from the Pacific Coast of Mexico and Southern California that was popularized by the legendary Ralph Rubio beginning in San Diego circa 1983. Rubio is considered the godfather of fish tacos. The fish or other seafood can be fried, grilled, or broiled. Fish tacos are usually served in soft flour or corn tortillas and garnished with cole slaw, pico de gallo and Mexican crema.

1 Before making the tortillas, ready all the ingredients for filling the tacos. Arrange in an assembly line. Keep heated fillings warm.

2 Press or shape and bake fresh Corn Tortillas (page 26 and 29) or Basic Flour Tortillas (page 31 and 32), or reheat store-bought tortillas (page 34). Keep warm (page 33).

3 Fill each taco shell with 2 tablespoons (28 g) of heated filling. Add 2 tablespoons (13 g) of Creamy, Spicy, Maybe Sweet Slaw and 1 tablespoon (16 g) of Pico de Gallo or chopped tomato. Top with 1 tablespoon (14 g) of Mexican crema or crème fraîche.

4 If making ahead for each diner to garnish, add the filling and keep the tacos warm in the oven until ready to serve. Cover tightly with foil to prevent drying out. Or wrap the tortillas individually, tightly in foil.

Q: *What does a depressed tortilla say?*
I don't want to taco 'bout it.

Breakfast Tacos

The term and popularity of "the breakfast taco" has become indelibly associated with Austin, Texas. The music-film-tech festival South by Southwest (SXSW) has had entertainment media flocking to the city since 1987. That's how the Breakfast Taco, as it has long been known in Austin, became a national thing. Writers and hipsters from Los Angeles and New York just couldn't get enough.

BREAKFAST TACOS

Makes 4 servings

8 (6- or 7-inch [15 or 18 cm]) Basic Flour Tortillas (page 50), or store-bought

2 cups (280 g) Scrambled Eggs (page 136)

2 cups (344 g) Refried Beans (page 83)

2 cups (450 g) Mexican-Style Breakfast Potatoes (page 139)

1 cup (80 g) grated cheddar, Colby, Colby Jack, Longhorn, Monterey Jack, Pepper Jack, or queso fresco (see What a Friend We Have in Cheeses, page 107)

Salsa(s), as desired (pages 101 to 105)

Flour tortillas are the default delivery system for breakfast tacos, although corn works as well. Still, flour tortillas define the genre. So, what's the difference between breakfast tacos and tacos to be eaten the rest of the time? The fillings. Breakfast tacos are distinguished by traditional breakfast fillings, starting with scrambled eggs. Add-ins often include bacon, breakfast sausage, chorizo, taco meat or ham, and perhaps fried potatoes or refried beans. Often, there's some cheese and, of course, a salsa to top things off.

And there's the fold. Breakfast tacos made with flour tortillas are folded at one end to stop fallout. Instead of the simple fold-over, the breakfast taco requires an open-ended burrito.

The size of the flour tortilla and the fold distinguish a breakfast taco from a breakfast burrito and burritos in general.

1 Preheat the oven to 350°F (180°C, or gas mark 4).

2 Before making the tortillas, ready all the ingredients for filling the tacos. Arrange in an assembly line. Keep heated fillings warm.

3 Press or shape and bake fresh Basic Flour Tortillas (page 31 and 32) or reheat store-bought tortillas (page 34). Keep warm (page 33).

4 Fill and roll each tortilla with ¼ cup (55 g) of filling and ¼ cup (30 g) of cheese. (See How to Roll a Breakfast Taco, opposite.)

5 Wrap the breakfast tacos individually in foil. Place in a baking dish or on a sheet pan. Or place the tacos in a shallow baking dish seam-side down. Cover tightly with foil. Place in the oven for 15 minutes or until heated through.

6 Serve with desired salsa(s).

HOW TO ROLL A BEAKFAST TACO

1 Place a (6- to 7-inch [15 or 18 cm]) flour tortilla on a cutting board or plate.

2 Arrange the fillings in the center from top to bottom.

3 Fold 1 side over the filling almost to the opposite edge.

4 Fold the other side over to make a cylinder.

5 Fold one end under.

6 That holds it together and keeps the filling inside—mostly.

SCRAMBLED EGGS FOR BREAKFAST TACOS AND BURRITOS

Makes 2 cups (280 g)

6 large eggs

4 tablespoons (60 ml) water, milk, or cream

1 teaspoon salt, or to taste

½ teaspoon freshly ground black pepper, or to taste

2 tablespoons (28 g) butter, (28 ml) vegetable oil, or combination, or cooking oil spray

The drier, the better is the usual formula for scrambled eggs to fill breakfast tacos. That's because soft scrambled eggs tend to make the tortilla soggy. Mixing water into beaten eggs makes the fluffiest, driest eggs. Adding milk or cream makes for a softer scramble. The choice is yours.

1 In a medium bowl using a whisk, fork, or electric beaters on low speed, beat the eggs until frothy, about 30 seconds.

2 Add water, milk, or cream and salt and pepper. Beat the eggs another 30 seconds or until well-blended.

3 Heat a large skillet or omelet pan over medium heat. The surface is ready when water sprinkled on the hot surface bubbles or "dances" and immediately evaporates. Add the butter or vegetable oil. Swirl the pan to evenly coat the bottoms and sides with melted butter or oil. Or lightly coat the bottom and sides with cooking oil spray.

4 Pour the beaten eggs into the pan all at once. Using a spatula, gently stir and cook the eggs for 2 to 3 minutes or until the eggs are set and crumbly.

5 Remove from the heat and keep warm.

Q:

Why is your pillow like a burrito?

Because its overstuffed.

ANYTHING BUT THE KITCHEN SINK

Leftovers, from meatloaf to pork roast to sautéed or grilled vegetables, make great stir-ins for breakfast taco scrambled eggs. Just chop and add to scrambled eggs: about 1 cup (225 g) (8 ounces) for 6 eggs.

ABOUT WRAPS

Since flour tortillas have become the new white bread, their versatility has spawned yet another genre of hand-held food: the wrap. The contemporary history of the wrap dates to 1982 and major league baseball manager Bobby Valentine. It is a story of improvisation in a moment of need, much like that of the nacho (Chapter 6).

Besides an illustrious career in baseball, Valentine is a successful restaurateur. It was at his first Bobby V's sports bar in his hometown of Stamford, Connecticut, that Valentine found himself in a squeeze play at lunch. One of his investors wanted his usual club sandwich on toast. The toaster was broken so Valentine wrapped the fillings for a club sandwich in a fresh tortilla with melted cheese on it. The investor loved it. So did the public after it went on the menu. Since then, the tortilla wrap has became as familiar as burgers in contemporary restaurants, sandwich shops, and delis. On supermarket shelves, packages of wraps are as plentiful as hamburger buns.

Wraps are thinner and larger in diameter than flour tortillas. Wraps are often flavored, more so than traditional tortillas. Flavored tortillas make great wraps. The fillings for wraps are usually more akin to those found in traditional sandwiches, such as roast beef, turkey, ham, tuna salad, and lettuce.

Of course, Middle Eastern traditions of wrapping fillings in flatbreads, known as lavash, predate contemporary wraps by a few thousand years. And the wrap is very similar to the burrito. Still, the modern wrap is its own thing.

In summary, to make a wrap instead of a burrito, put sandwich ingredients in an oversize flour tortilla. Roll and enjoy.

Scrambled Eggs with Sausage for Breakfast Tacos: Crumble ½ pound (225 g) of uncooked bulk breakfast sausage into a large skillet heated over medium heat. Cook and stir the sausage for 3 minutes or until no longer pink. Continue to cook for another 3 to 5 minutes or until as brown and crisp as desired. Drain the sausage on paper towels. Stir into the beaten eggs and proceed with step 4 on the opposite page.

Scrambled Eggs with Bacon for Breakfast Tacos: Stack 6 strips of uncooked bacon. Using a sharp knife, cut the bacon into 1-inch (2.5 cm) pieces. Place the bacon pieces in a large skillet heated over medium heat. Cook and stir the bacon for about 3 minutes or until no longer pink. Cook for another 3 to 5 minutes or until as brown and as crisp as desired. Drain the bacon on paper towels. Stir into the beaten eggs and proceed with step 4 on the opposite page.

Scrambled Eggs with Chorizo for Breakfast Tacos: Crumble ½ pound (225 g) of uncooked Homemade Chorizo (page 72) (or use store-bought chorizo) into a large skillet heated over medium heat. Cook and stir the chorizo for about 3 minutes or until no longer pink. Cook for another 3 to 5 minutes or until as brown and as crisp as desired. Drain the chorizo on paper towels. Stir into the beaten eggs, and proceed with step 4 on the opposite page.

Scrambled Eggs with Ground Beef Filling for Breakfast Tacos: Crumble ½ pound (225 g) of uncooked Ground Beef Filling (page 68) into a large skillet heated over medium heat. Cook and stir the Ground Beef Filling for about 3 minutes or until no longer pink. Cook for another 3 to 5 minutes or until as brown and as crisp as desired. Drain the Ground Beef Filling on paper towels. Stir into the beaten eggs and proceed with step 4 on the opposite page.

Scrambled Eggs with Ham, Steak, Brisket or Other Cooked Filling: Chop, shred, or slice 1 cup (225 g) or 8 ounces of cooked filling into 1-inch (2.5 cm) pieces. Add to a large skillet heated over medium heat. Cook and stir, just to heat through, about 2 to 3 minutes. Proceed with step 4 on the opposite page.

MEXICAN-STYLE BREAKFAST POTATOES

Makes 2 cups (450 g)

1½ pounds (680 g) russet (peeled), red (unpeeled), or white (unpeeled) potatoes, cut into ½-inch (13 mm) pieces

Water, for cooking potatoes

2 tablespoons (28 ml) vegetable oil or bacon grease

½ cup (80 g) thin-sliced white or yellow onion (optional)

1 teaspoon salt, or to taste

⅛ teaspoon cayenne pepper (optional)

These are great as a filling for Breakfast Tacos (page 134) or as a side with egg dishes, see Mexican Breakfast (page 145). Adding proteins to the potatoes makes for a particularly satisfying side dish (see below).

1 In a medium saucepan over high heat, add the potatoes and enough water to cover. Bring to a boil. Lower the heat and simmer, uncovered, for 8 minutes. Do not cook the potatoes until tender. We are parcooking.

2 Drain the potatoes in a colander. Run cool water over the potatoes for 1 minute to stop the cooking process.

3 In a large skillet over medium high heat, warm the vegetable oil or bacon grease until it shimmers, about 1 minute.

4 Add the onion, cooking and stirring for about 2 minutes or until the onion is translucent and soft but not browned.

5 Add the potatoes, salt and pepper. Stir gently. Cook for about 3 minutes or until browned on one side. Stir and cook for another 1 to 2 minutes or until brown and easily pierced with a fork.

Breakfast Potatoes with Sausage, Chorizo, Ground Beef, Bacon, or Ham: Stir in 1 cup (225 g) of cooked, crumbled bulk sausage, (225 g) Homemade Chorizo (page 72) or Ground Beef Filling (page 68); or 1 cup (80 g) of chopped, crisp-cooked bacon; or 1 cup (150 g) of diced ham along with the potatoes, as with step 5 above.

MOVIES WITH "TORTILLA" IN THE TITLE

- *Tortilla Flat*, 1942, based on the John Steinbeck novel of the same name.
- *Tortilla Soup*, 2001, romantic comedy where food is the love potion.
- *Tortilla Heaven*, 2008, about a miracle tortilla.

Burritos

The defining characteristic of a burrito is the flour tortilla. Burritos are always made with flour tortillas. The Mexican burrito dates to the early 1900s and the northern state of Chihuahua where wheat grows more easily than corn. Popular legend has it that a food merchant, Juan Mendez, in the town of Juarez, across the border from El Paso, started wrapping his prepared food in large flour tortillas, then in a napkin, to keep the food warm. He sold the bundles out of his donkey cart and eventually the offering became known as a burrito, or "little donkey." Although the creation story seems to lead to the conclusion that the modern burrito is a Tex-Mex thing, this is not so.

The huge, overstuffed flour tortilla exemplified by the Chipotle model today became popular in the early 60s in the Mission district of San Francisco—hence its designation as the Mission burrito. Even bigger and stuffed with more stuff, the Mission burrito was wrapped in foil to keep it warm. That is why what we know as a burrito today is more of a California thing. California marketers, like Taco Bell and Chipotle, outbrand Texans when it comes to mass Mexican food.

BURRITOS

Makes 4 servings

4 (10 to 12 inches, or 25 to 30 cm) Basic Flour Tortillas (page 50), or store-bought

2 cups (450 g) or a combination of heated fillings, such as:
• Ground Beef (page 68)
• Shredded Beef Brisket (page 69)
• Carne Guisada (Mexican Beef Stew) (page 177)
• Fajitas, Beef or Chicken (page 70)

• Puerco Guisada (Red Chile Pork Stew) (page 178)
• Carnitas (page 71)
• Shredded Spicy Chicken (page 74)
• Shredded Roast Duck (page 75)
• Shrimp or Crab (page 76)
• Pinto Beans (page 80)
• Black Beans (page 81)
• Refried Pinto or Black Beans (page 83)

1 cup (120 g) grated cheddar, Colby, Colby Jack, Longhorn, Monterey Jack, Pepper Jack, or (150 g) queso fresco (see What a Friend We Have in Cheeses, page 107.)

2 cups (550 g) heated sauce (optional):
• Tex-Mex Chili Gravy (page 90)
• New Mexico Red Chilli Sauce (page 91)

• Tomato and Green Chile Sauce (page 92)
• Green Tomatillo Sauce (page 93)
• Roasted Tomatillo Sauce (page 93)
• Real Deal Mole (page 94)
• Easier Mole (page 96)
• Sour Cream Enchilada Sauce (page 97)
• Queso (page 99)

Q:
What do penguins eat?
Brrrrritos.

This is the recipe for a basic burrito, filled and stuffed. What goes into a burrito, like a taco, is only limited by your imagination and what you are willing to buy and cook. That said, we'll stick to the delicious fillings in Chapter 5. But go ahead and spread your burrito wings—experiment. When contemplating options, reference the combinations for enchiladas in Chapter 8 (page 151).

One of the attributes of a properly folded burrito is that is can hold "wet" fillings, like the meaty stews *carne* or *puerco guisada.*

Burritos have multiple identifies. They can be baked and sauced much like an enchilada. They can be fried and sauced or not. In that guise, a burrito becomes a chimichanga.

continued

continued

1   Preheat the oven to 350°F (180°C, or gas mark 4).

2   Press or shape and bake fresh Basic Flour Tortillas (page 31 and 32), or reheat store-bought flour tortillas (page 34). Keep warm (page 33).

3   Fill and roll each tortilla with ½ cup (113 g) of desired filling and ¼ cup (30 g) of cheese. See How to Roll a Burrito (below).

4   Wrap the burritos individually in foil, seam-side down. Place in a baking dish or on a sheet pan. Or place the burritos in a shallow baking dish seam-side down. Cover tightly with foil. Place in the oven for 15 minutes or until heated through.

5   If desired, top each burrito with heated sauce and sprinkle with an additional 1 tablespoon (8 g) of cheese. Optional: Return to the oven to melt the cheese, about 5 minutes.

Chimichangas: After filling and rolling the burritos (step 2), heat 2 inches (5 cm) of vegetable oil in a deep fryer or electric skillet to 375°F (190°C). Or use a deep skillet or other large pot over medium heat and a candy/frying thermometer. To make sure the chimichanga doesn't come undone, secure the seams with toothpicks. Carefully lower the chimichangas, 1 at a time, into the hot oil. Cook for about 1 minute or until crisp and golden brown. Turn and cook for another minute or until crisp and golden brown on all sides. Drain on paper towels. Keep warm. Repeat with the remaining chimichangas. If desired, serve with the desired sauce spooned over the top and a sprinkling of cheese.

HOW TO ROLL A BURRITO OR WRAP

1   Place an oversize (10- to 12-inch [25 to 30 cm]) flour tortilla on a cutting board or plate.

2   Arrange the fillings in the center from top to bottom.

3   Fold the sides halfway over the filling. Leave room for the filling to spread out.

4   Fold the bottom a third of the way up.

5   Now, roll the whole thing up. Press down gently to seal.

6   If desired, lightly griddle to warm the filling and melt the cheese.

BREAKFAST BURRITOS

Makes 4 servings

4 (10 to 12- inch [25 to 30 cm]) Basic Flour Tortillas (page 50), or store-bought

2 cups (280 g) Scrambled Eggs (page 136)

1 cup (172 g) Refried Beans (page 83)

2 cups (450 g) Mexican-Style Breakfast Potatoes (page 139)

1 cup (120 g) grated cheddar, Colby, Colby Jack, Longhorn, Monterey Jack, Pepper Jack, or (150 g) queso fresco (see What a Friend We Have in Cheeses, page 107)

2 cups (550 g) heated sauce (optional):
• Tex-Mex Chili Gravy (page 90)
• New Mexico Red Chile Sauce (page 91)
• Tomato and Green Chilli Sauce (page 92)
• Green Tomatillo Sauce (page 93)
• Roasted Tomatillo Sauce (page 93)
• Queso (page 99)

Salsa as desired (page 101 to 104)

These are breakfast tacos on steroids. They start with larger flour tortillas, heavily stuffed with breakfast ingredients. For additional "yum," try toasting a breakfast burrito in butter.

1 Preheat the oven to 350ºF (180ºC, or gas mark 4).

2 Press or shape and bake fresh Basic Flour Tortillas (page 31 and 32), or reheat store-bought tortillas (page 34). Keep warm (page 33).

3 Fill and roll each tortilla with ½ cup (112 g) desired filling and ¼ (30 g) cup of cheese. (See How to Roll a Burrito, opposite.)

4 Wrap the burritos individually in foil, seam side down. Place in a baking dish or on a sheet pan. Or place the burritos in a shallow baking dish seam-side down. Cover tightly with foil. Place in the oven for 15 minutes or until heated through.

5 If desired, top each burrito with heated sauce and sprinkle with an additional 1 tablespoon (8 g) of cheese. Return to the oven to melt the cheese, about 5 minutes.

Toasted Breakfast Burritos: After filling and rolling the burritos (step 2), heat a comal or griddle over medium heat. The surface is ready when water sprinkled on the hot surface bubbles or "dances" and immediately evaporates. For each burrito, melt 1 tablespoon (14 g) of butter until bubbly. Place the burrito seam-side down in the butter. Cook for about 1 minute or until golden brown. Turn and cook for another 1 to 2 minutes until golden brown. Repeat with the remaining burritos. If desired, serve with the desired sauce spooned over the top and a sprinkling of cheese.

Q: *Why did the burrito blush?*
It saw the salad dressing.

Mexican Breakfast

As we've seen, tortillas aren't just for lunch and dinner. Mexican breakfast is a specific meal in the Southwest. It means a choice of several egg dishes made with tortillas. Instead of toast, more tortillas—usually flour—are served as well. It's a tortilla-intense meal.

We've already focused on breakfast tacos and burritos. Now, we'll make gorditas, a special Texas-Mexico border breakfast treat, and Mexican-style egg dishes that use tortillas.

GORDITAS (MEXICAN PITA)

Makes 4 servings

12 Gorditas (page 47), warm

2 cups (450 g) filling, such as:
• Spicy Chicken (page 74)
• Braised Pork (page 71)
• Carnitas (page 71)

• Homemade Chorizo (page 72)
• Carne Guisada (page 177)
• Puerco Guisada (page 178)
• Refried Beans (page 83)
• Scrambled Eggs (page 136)

• Breakfast Potatoes (page 139)
• or a combination of fillings

2 cups (300 g) shredded queso fresco or -(160 g) cotija (see What a Friend We Have in Cheeses, page 107)

1 cup (260 g) Red Salsa (page 101) or Green Tomatillo Salsa (page 102)

Gorditas are the Mexican equivalent of pita pockets, and they are a huge breakfast tradition, particularly in South Texas, where they are sold in restaurants, supermarket delis, and convenience stores.

These are for eating out of hand, but feel free to use a knife and fork. And a Red or Green Tomatillo Salsa makes a great finishing touch. Gorditas (which means "fat little ones") are made from corn masa. Instead of being pressed as flat as a tortilla, gorditas are thicker and after baking, and are usually split like a pita for filling—though if you make them a couple inches larger, you can fold them and make thick tacos. Often, gorditas may contain a combination of fillings, such as scrambled eggs and potatoes or chorizo and refried beans.

1   Split a gordita as you would pita, leaving a closed bottom seam. Do not cut all the way through. If it splits, don't sweat it. Treat it like a mini English muffin. Fill and eat.

2   Fill with 2 tablespoons (28 g) of the desired filling(s). Top with 2 tablespoons (10 to 19 g) of the desired cheese. Keep warm and serve immediately.

3   Pass the salsa for garnishing, about 1 tablespoon (16 g) per gordita.

CHILAQUILES (TORTILLA PIECES WITH GREEN TOMATILLO SAUCE)

Makes 6 servings

3 cups (735 g) Green Tomatillo Sauce (page 93)

2 tablespoons (28 ml), plus 2 cups (475 ml) vegetable oil

½ cup (80 g) chopped white or yellow onions

12 Corn Tortillas (page 38), or store-bought, cut into 1-inch (2.5 cm) squares

1 cup (150 g) shredded queso fresco or (115 g) Monterey Jack cheese (see What a Friend We Have in Cheeses, page 107)

No doubt this dish was developed to use leftover corn tortillas. It is doubtful that you will ever have leftover homemade tortillas. So don't feel guilty about using store-bought corn tortillas to make chilaquiles. This vibrant breakfast dish is often served as a side with Scrambled Eggs (page 136). Tortilla pieces may be fried crisp or sautéed soft.

1 In a large saucepan over medium heat, bring the Green Tomatillo Sauce to a slow boil. Lower the heat and simmer for 20 minutes or until slightly thickened. Set aside and keep warm.

2 In a large skillet over medium high heat, warm 2 tablespoons (28 ml) of oil until it shimmers. Add the onions and cook for 3 minutes, or until translucent and soft but not brown. Add the onions to the Green Tomatillo Sauce. Keep warm.

3 In the same skillet over medium-high heat, warm the remaining 2 cups (475 ml) of oil to 350°F (180°C).

4 For crispy tortilla pieces: When the oil is hot, carefully slide half of the tortilla squares into the oil and fry for 1 to 2 minutes or until light golden and crisp. Using a skimmer or slotted spoon, remove the fried tortilla pieces and place on paper towels to drain. Repeat with the remaining tortilla pieces.

5 For sautéed tortilla pieces: In a large skillet over medium heat, warm ¼ cup (60 ml) of vegetable oil. Stir in half of the tortilla squares, stirring and cooking for 2 to 3 minutes or until soft and crispy at the edges. Using a skimmer or slotted spoon, remove the fried tortilla pieces and place on paper towels to drain. Repeat with the remaining tortilla pieces.

6 Discard the oil and wipe the skillet clean. Return the fried tortilla pieces to the skillet. Pour the sauce over the crispy tortilla pieces to cover.

7 Sprinkle with the cheese. Serve immediately.

MIGAS (SCRAMBLED EGGS WITH TORTILLAS, ONIONS, PEPPERS, AND TOMATOES)

Makes 4 servings

6 Corn Tortillas (page 38), or store-bought, cut into 1-inch (2.5 cm) squares

2 cups (475 ml) plus 1 tablespoon (15 ml) vegetable oil or ¼ cup (60 ml) vegetable oil

½ cup (80 g) chopped white or yellow onion

1 tablespoon (9 g) chopped jalapeño, stemed and seeded

½ cup (90 g) chopped tomato, rinsed and drained

6 large eggs, lightly beaten

1 cup (112 g) shredded cheddar, Colby, Colby Jack, Longhorn, Monterey Jack, Pepper Jack, or (150 g) queso fresco (see What a Friend We Have in Cheeses, page 107)

This dish is a first cousin to Chilaquiles (page 146). Fried or sautéed tortilla pieces, along with tomatoes, sautéed onions and chillies, are stirred into scrambled eggs. Tortillas may be fried until crispy or sautéed just to soften and crisp the edges. It's another dish that likely originated as a use for leftover or slightly stale corn tortillas.

1 **For crispy tortilla pieces:** In an electric skillet or large skillet over medium-high heat, warm 2 cups (475 ml) of oil to 350°F (180°C). When the oil is hot, carefully slide half of the tortilla squares into the oil and fry for 1 to 2 minutes or until light golden and crisp. Using a skimmer or slotted spoon, remove the fried tortilla pieces and place on paper towels to drain. Repeat with the remaining tortilla pieces.

For sautéed tortilla pieces: In a large skillet over medium high heat, warm ¼ cup (60 ml) of vegetable oil. Stir in half of the tortilla squares, stirring and cooking for 2 to 3 minutes or until soft and crispy at the edges. Using a skimmer or slotted spoon, remove the fried tortilla pieces and place on paper towels to drain. Repeat with the remaining tortilla pieces.

2 Pour off all but 1 tablespoon (15 ml) of oil. Return the skillet to medium heat. Add the onion and cook until soft but not brown, about 3 minutes. Stir in the jalapeño and cook for 30 seconds. Add the tomato and cook for 1 minute or just until the tomatoes are heated through.

3 Place the tortilla pieces in the pan, stirring to combine with the vegetables.

4 Reduce the heat to low. Pour the beaten eggs over the mixture and cook over low heat for 2 to 3 minutes or until the eggs are set.

5 During the last minute of cooking, sprinkle the cheese over the eggs. When the cheese is melted, the eggs are ready to serve immediately.

HUEVOS RANCHEROS (FRIED EGGS ON TORTILLAS WITH TOMATO AND GREEN CHILE SAUCE)

Makes 4 servings

½ cup (1 stick or 112 g) unsalted butter, divided use

4 tablespoons (60 ml) vegetable oil, divided use

8 Corn Tortillas (page 38), or store-bought, heated (page 34)

8 large eggs

2 cups (490 g) Tomato and Green Chile Sauce (page 92), warm

This is a Mexican food riff on Eggs Benedict. A piquant sauce over fried eggs on tortillas is the legendary breakfast dish of Mexico and border states. Eggs for Huevos Rancheros should be cooked sunny side and no more done than medium so that the soft yellow yolk, when pierced with a fork, runs and blends with the red and green sauce. It is traditionally served with Refried Beans (page 83), and Breakfast Potatoes (page 139), but try it with black beans as well.

1   Preheat the oven to 300ºF (150ºC, or gas mark 2). Warm 4 large, ovenproof dinner plates in the oven while heating.

2   In a large skillet over medium heat, warm 2 tablespoons (28 g) of butter for about 1 minute or until the butter sizzles. Add 1 tablespoon (15 ml) of vegetable oil, stirring to combine.

3   Using tongs, add 2 tortillas to the butter and oil. Cook on one side, about 30 seconds or just until the edges curl. Turn and cook for another 20 seconds. Lift the tortillas out of the skillet, allowing any excess oil to drain back into the pan. Place the tortillas on a heated plate, with the edges slightly overlapping.

4   Into a small dish, break 2 eggs, being careful not to pierce the yolks. Carefully pour the eggs into the skillet and cover with a tight-fitting lid. Cook over low heat for 2 to 4 minutes, depending on whether you want the eggs very soft or medium.

5   Using a large spatula, lift the eggs onto the sautéed tortillas. Pour ½ cup (138 g) of Tomato and Green Chile Sauce over the eggs. Keep warm in the oven while cooking the remaining tortillas and eggs in the same way. Serve immediately.

8

MAIN FRAMES: ENCHILADAS, FAJITAS, AND TACO SALADS

In this category of dishes, tortillas are wrapped, rolled, and molded to hold fillings. Enchiladas are corn tortillas rolled around fillings that are then sauced and baked. Fajitas are flour tortillas wrapped around strips of grilled beef or chicken and other good stuff. The contemporary fast-food driven image of the taco salad is that of a giant flour tortilla fried into the shape of a crisp, edible bowl. It's a gimmick, but a successful one.

Enchiladas

Few dishes are more comforting than enchiladas. Whether they are Mexican, Tex-Mex, New Mexico-style Mexican, Sonoran (Arizona)–style Mexican, or Cal-Mex, enchiladas are the knife-and-fork symbol of tortilla cuisine just as tacos are the handheld icon.

Enchiladas can be traditional, simple *campesino* cuisine or sophisticated and updated. There are as many versions of enchilada combinations as there are cooks who make them. Enchiladas may be made with white, yellow, or blue—or any color and any flavor—corn tortillas. But, to be an enchilada, the tortilla should be corn. Enchiladas may be rolled, the more familiar technique, though enchiladas also come in stacks, particularly in New Mexico and West Texas. Enchiladas usually come with sides of beans and rice. A dollop of guacamole never hurts.

The enchilada recipes that follow provide instructions for both techniques. Note these are guidelines for your enchilada creativity. Each recipe represents the options for a particular classification of filling, starting with beef, with various sauce and cheese options. Other kinds of enchiladas start with chicken, pork, cheese, and vegetables fillings, with options. These recipes make four servings.

Let your palate be your guide.

Q: *When does an enchilada get smothered with cheese?*
In the best queso scenario.

HOW TO SOFTEN CORN TORTILLAS FOR ENCHILADAS

In a small skillet over medium heat, warm ½ inch (13 mm) of vegetable oil until it shimmers. Using tongs, place 1 corn tortilla into the hot oil for about 10 seconds. Turn the tortilla and cook for about 10 seconds longer or until the edges flutter and the tortilla floats. Place the softened tortilla on a plate or pie pan. Repeat until all the tortillas are softened, stacking the tortillas.

BEEF ENCHILADAS

Makes 12 rolled or 4 stacked enchiladas (4 servings)

12 Corn Tortillas (page 38), or store-bought, softened (page 34)

3 cups (675 g) Ground Beef Filling (page 68), heated

3 cups (525 g) heated Tex-Mex Chili Gravy (page 90), New Mexico Red Chile Sauce (page 91), Sour Cream Enchilada Sauce (page 97), Tomato and Green Chile Sauce (page 92), or Queso (page 99)

1 cup (112 g) shredded cheese, such as cheddar, Colby, Colby Jack, Monterey Jack, Pepper Jack, or queso fresco

Seasoned Ground Beef Filling is the traditional beef enchilada filling. Tex-Mex Chili Gravy and Red Chile Sauce are the traditional sauces. Yellow cheese usually goes on top. Shredded Beef Brisket (page 153) and Fajitas Beef (page 70) are also great fillings for enchiladas.

1 Preheat the oven to 350°F (180°C, or gas mark 4). Spray a (9 x 11-inch [23 x 33 cm]) baking dish with cooking spray.

2 **For Rolled Enchiladas:** Place about ¼ cup (56 g) filling in the center of a tortilla. Roll and place seam-side down in the baking dish. Repeat until all the tortillas are filled, arranging them in the baking dish. Pour the sauce over the enchiladas. Make sure the sauce runs between the enchiladas.

For Stacked Enchiladas: Arrange 4 softened tortillas in single layer in one large or two small baking dishes. Place about ⅓ cup (75 g) of filling in the center of each tortilla, spreading the filling evenly toward the edges. Repeat with another softened tortilla and ⅓ cup (75 g) of filling. Top with a third softened tortilla. Repeat to make four stacks. Pour the sauce over the enchiladas. Make sure the sauce entirely coats the top of each stacked enchilada and runs down the sides.

3 Sprinkle the tops of the enchiladas with shredded cheese.

4 Place in the oven for 15 minutes, until the cheese is melted and the sauce is bubbly. Serve immediately.

PORK ENCHILADAS

Makes 12 rolled or
4 stacked enchiladas
(4 servings)

12 Corn Tortillas
(page 38), or store-
bought, softened
(page 34)

3 cups (720 g)
Carnitas or Braised
Pork (page 71),
heated

3 cups (735 g)
heated Green
Tomatillo Sauce
(page 93), Tomato
and Green Chile
Sauce (page 92),
New Mexico Red
Chile Sauce (page
91), Real Deal Mole
(page 94), or Easier
Mole (page 96)

1 cup (115 g)
shredded Monterey
jack

Puerco enchilada fillings are more common in Mexico but shouldn't be discounted north of the border where we are more likely to think of pork as the inside of a tamale or a street taco. Carnitas are classic inside an enchilada. Top with a tangy vegetable sauce and use white cheese.

As an alternative, use shredded pork with New Mexico Red Chile Sauce (page 91) and yellow cheese.

1 Preheat the oven to 350ºF (180ºC, or gas mark 4). Spray a (9 x 11-inch [23 x 33]) baking dish with cooking spray.

2 **For Rolled Enchiladas**: Place about ¼ cup (60 g) of filling in the center of a tortilla. Roll and place seam-side down in the baking dish. Repeat until all the tortillas are filled, arranging them in the baking dish. Pour the sauce over the enchiladas. Make sure the sauce runs between the enchiladas.

For Stacked Enchiladas: Arrange 4 softened tortillas in a single layer in one large or two small baking dishes. Place about ⅓ cup (80 g) of filling in the center of each tortilla, spreading filling evenly toward the edges. Repeat with another softened tortilla and ⅓ cup (80 g) of filling. Top with a third softened tortilla. Repeat to make four stacks. Pour the sauce over enchiladas. Make sure the sauce entirely coats the top of each stacked enchilada and runs down the sides.

3 Sprinkle the tops of the enchiladas with shredded cheese.

4 Place in the oven for 15 minutes, until the cheese is melted and the sauce is bubbly. Serve immediately.

Q: *A pair of enchiladas are in the microwave. One says "Wow, it's hot in here." The other replies, "Oh my gosh, a talking enchilada!"*

CHICKEN ENCHILADAS

Makes 12 rolled or 4 stacked enchiladas (4 servings)

12 Corn Tortillas (page 38), or store-bought, softened (page 34)

3 cups (375 g) Spicy Chicken (page 74), Fajita Chicken (page 70), or Roast Duck (page 75) heated

3 cups (735 g) heated Green Tomatillo Sauce (page 93), Real Deal Mole Sauce (page 94), Easier Mole Sauce (page 96), Sour Cream Enchilada Sauce (page 97), New Mexico Red Chile Sauce (page 91), or Roasted Tomatillo Sauce (page 93), Tomato and Green Chile Sauce (page 92)

1 cup (115 g) shredded Monterey Jack cheese

1 cup (230 g) Avocado Crema (page 106) (optional)

Unlike beef, chicken is a favorite filling in Mexico and it's popular on both sides of the border. Often, green, mole, and white sauces are used to top chicken enchiladas. Often, the cheese is white, as well.

This is the category where we'll put Fajita Chicken and Roast Duck alternatives, along with sauces and cheeses for each. Try a spoonful of Avocado Crema (page 106) on top of any of these.

1 Preheat the oven to 350°F (180°C, or gas mark 4). Spray a (9 x 11-inch [23 x 33 cm]) baking dish with cooking spray.

2 For Rolled Enchiladas: Place about ¼ cup (31 g) of filling in the center of a tortilla. Roll and place seam-side down in the baking dish. Repeat until all the tortillas are filled, arranging them in baking dish. Pour the sauce over the enchiladas. Make sure the sauce runs between the enchiladas.

For Stacked Enchiladas: Arrange 4 softened tortillas in single layer in the baking dishes. Place about ⅓ cup (42 g) of filling in the center of each tortilla, spreading the filling evenly toward the edges. Repeat with another softened tortilla and ⅓ cup (42 g) of filling. Top with a third softened tortilla. Repeat to make four stacks. Pour the sauce over the enchiladas. Make sure the sauce entirely coats the top of each stacked enchilada and runs down the sides.

3 Sprinkle the tops of the enchiladas with shredded cheese.

4 Place in the oven for 15 minutes, until the cheese is melted and the sauce is bubbly. If desired, drizzle with Avocado Crema. Serve immediately.

PUT AN EGG ON IT

A classic Rio Grande border or New Mexico garnish for stacked enchiladas is a soft fried egg. Bake the enchiladas and keep warm while frying 1 egg per stack.

Q:
What tortilla dish is good at math?
Inch-iladas.

SHRIMP OR CRAB ENCHILADAS

Makes 12 rolled or
4 stacked enchiladas
(4 servings)

**12 Corn Tortillas
(page 38), or store-
bought, softened
(page 34)**

**2 cups (650 g)
Shrimp or Crab
(page 76), heated**

**2 cups (230 g)
shredded Monterey
Jack cheese, divided
use**

**3 cups (525 g)
heated Green
Tomatillo Sauce
(page 93), Tomato
and Green Chile
Sauce (page
92), Sour Cream
Enchilada Sauce
(page 97), or Queso
(page 99);**

**Pico de Gallo
(page 104)**

Seafood has become an increasingly popular enchilada filling. Adding some cheese helps hold the seafood together. Saucing with a piquant sauce provides a nice flavor and texture contrast. Black Beans and Green Rice are the traditional sidekicks to tortillas with seafood fillings. Serve with Pico de Gallo, as well.

1 Preheat the oven to 350°F (180°C, or gas mark 4). Spray a (9 x 11-inch [23 x 33 cm]) baking dish with cooking spray.

2 **For Rolled Enchiladas**: Place 3 tablespoons (60 g) of shrimp or crab and 2 tablespoons (14 g) of cheese in the center of a tortilla. Roll and place seam-side down in the baking dish. Repeat until all the tortillas are filled, arranging them in the baking dish. Pour the sauce over the enchiladas. Make sure the sauce runs between the enchiladas.

For Stacked Enchiladas: Arrange 4 softened tortillas in single layer in two baking dishes. Place about 3 tablespoon (60 g) of filling and 3 tablespoons (21 g) of cheese in the center of each tortilla, spreading the filling evenly toward the edges. Repeat with another softened tortilla and fillings. Top with a third softened tortilla. Repeat to make four stacks. Pour the sauce over the enchiladas. Make sure the sauce entirely coats the top of each stacked enchilada and runs down the sides.

3 Sprinkle the tops of the enchiladas with the remaining shredded cheese.

4 Place in the oven for 15 minutes, until the cheese is melted and the sauce is bubbly. Serve immediately.

5 Serve with Pico de Gallo, if desired.

CHEESE ENCHILADAS

Makes 12 rolled or
4 stacked enchiladas
(4 servings)

3 cups (345 g)
shredded cheddar,
Colby, Colby Jack, or
Longhorn cheese,
plus 1 cup (115 g) for
garnish

12 Corn Tortillas
(page 38), or store-
bought, softened
(page 34)

3 cups (825 g)
heated Tex-Mex Chili
Gravy (page 90),
New Mexico Red
Chile Sauce
(page 91), Queso
(page 99)

For some, there's no way to have too much cheese on a pizza. Some enchilada aficionados feel the same. Stuff an enchilada with yellow cheese and top it with Queso. Or top with a New Mexico Red Chile Sauce or Tex-Mex Chili Gravy. You can experiment with other cheeses for fillings and sauces as well. Any of these would be great with Chipotle Salsa.

To go old school Tex-Mex, sprinkle finely chopped white onion on top of the Tex-Mex Chili Gravy just before serving.

1 Preheat the oven to 350ºF (180ºC, or gas mark 4). Spray a 9 x 11-inch (23 x 33 cm) baking dish with cooking spray.

2 **For Rolled Enchiladas:** Place about ¼ cup (29 g) of filling in the center of a tortilla. Roll and place seam side down in the baking dish. Repeat until all the tortillas are filled, arranging them in baking dish. Pour the sauce over the enchiladas. Make sure the sauce runs between the enchiladas.

For Stacked Enchiladas: Arrange 4 softened tortillas in single layer in one large or two smaller baking dishes. Place about ⅓ cup (38 g) of filling in the center of each tortilla, spreading the filling evenly toward the edges. Repeat with another softened tortilla and ⅓ cup (38 g) of filling. Top with a third softened tortilla. Repeat to make four stacks. Pour the sauce over the enchiladas. Make sure the sauce entirely coats the top of each stacked enchilada and runs down the sides.

3 Sprinkle the tops of the enchiladas with shredded cheese.

4 Place in the oven for 15 minutes, until the cheese is melted and the sauce is bubbly. Serve immediately.

BEAN ENCHILADAS

Makes 12 rolled or
4 stacked enchiladas
(4 servings)

12 Corn Tortillas (page 38), or store-bought, softened (page 34)

2 cups (344 g) Refried Pinto (page 83) or Refried Black Beans (page 83)

1 cup (172 g) well-drained Pinto (page 80) or Black Beans (page 81)

1 cup (225 g) shredded cheddar or Monterey Jack cheese, divided use

3 cups (825) heated Tex-Mex Chili Gravy (page 90), New Mexico Red Chile Sauce (page 91), Tomato and Green Chile Sauce (page 92), Roasted Tomatillo Sauce (page 93), Queso (page 99)

Pinto beans and yellow cheese; black beans and white cheese—that's usually the way it goes. Bean fillings beg for flavored, beautifully colored tortillas. For this soft filling, stacked enchiladas are the best.

1 Preheat the oven to 350ºF (180ºC, or gas mark 4). Spray a 9 x 11-inch (23 x 33 cm) baking dish with cooking spray.

2 In a medium bowl, stir together the refried beans and whole beans to use as filling.

3 For Rolled Enchiladas: Place about ¼ cup (60 g) of filling in the center of a tortilla. Roll and place seam-side down in the baking dish. Repeat until all the tortillas are filled, arranging them in baking dish. Pour the sauce over the enchiladas. Make sure the sauce runs between the enchiladas.

For Stacked Enchiladas: Arrange 4 softened tortillas in single layer in one large or two small baking dishes. Place about ⅓ cup (80 g) of filling in the center of each tortilla, spreading the filling evenly toward the edges. Repeat with another softened tortilla and ⅓ cup (80 g) of filling. Top with a third softened tortilla. Repeat to make four stacks. 4. Pour sauce over enchiladas. Make sure the sauce entirely coats the top of each stacked enchilada and runs down the sides.

4 Sprinkle the tops of the enchiladas with shredded cheese.

5 Place in the oven for 15 minutes, until the cheese is melted and the sauce is bubbly. Serve immediately.

VEGGIE ENCHILADAS

Makes 12 rolled or
4 stacked enchiladas

4 cups (120 g) fresh spinach or (480 g) coarsely chopped zucchini or summer squash plus 2 tablespoons (28 ml) vegetable oil

2 cups (140 g) sliced mushrooms

2½ cups (288 g) shredded Monterey Jack or Pepper Jack cheese, divided use

12 Corn Tortillas (page 30), or store-bought, softened (page 34)

3 cups (825 g) heated Green Tomatillo Sauce (page 93), Tomato and Green Chile Sauce (page 93), Sour Cream Enchilada Sauce (page 97), or Queso (page 99)

Make the most of this meatless option. Go for lots of flavor with one of the tangy tomatillo sauces or go creamy with Sour Cream Enchilada Sauce or Queso.

1 Preheat the oven to 350ºF (180ºC, or gas mark 4). Spray a 9 x 11-inch (23 x 33 cm) baking dish with cooking spray.

2 In a large skillet over medium heat, combine the spinach or squash, vegetable oil, and mushrooms. Cook until the spinach is wilted or the squash and mushrooms are soft, about 3 to 5 minutes. You should have about 3 cups (720 g) of cooked vegetables.

3 **For Rolled Enchiladas:** Place about ¼ cup (60 g) of vegetables and 2 tablespoons (14 g) of cheese in the center of a tortilla. Roll and place seam-side down in the baking dish. Repeat until all the tortillas are filled, arranging them in the baking dish. Pour the sauce over the enchiladas. Make sure the sauce runs between the enchiladas.

For Stacked Enchiladas: Arrange 4 softened tortillas in single layer in one large or two small baking dishes. Place about ⅓ cup (80 g) of vegetables and 3 tablespoons (21 g) of cheese in the center of each tortilla, spreading the filling evenly toward the edges. Repeat with another softened tortilla and ⅓ cup (80 g) of filling. Top with a third softened tortilla. Repeat to make four stacks. Pour the sauce over the enchiladas. Make sure the sauce entirely coats the top of each stacked enchilada and runs down the side.

4 Sprinkle the tops of the enchiladas with the remaning shredded cheese.

5 Bake for 15 minutes, until the cheese is melted and the sauce is bubbly. Serve immediately.

Fajitas

In the beginning, fajitas were beef. South Texas and Northern Mexico ranch hands grilled the less tender cut, known as skirt steak, over indigenous mesquite wood coals because *el jefe* (the boss man) didn't want it (the meat or the mesquite). The skirt steak was cut into strips and wrapped in flour tortillas.

In the 1970s, this dish became restaurant fare and popular way beyond Houston, where restaurateur and South Texas native, "Mama Ninfa" Laurenzo, introduced fajitas beyond Rio Grande ranches.

Now, the price of skirt steak has grown, along with the popularity of this DIY entrée. Also, as the popularity of fajitas has grown, the term has come to include marinated, grilled, and thin-sliced strips of chicken, as well just about anything, including shrimp (page 76). Or go vegetarian using assorted grilled vegetables of your choice.

Fajitas are best when the meat and veggies are grilled. But pan- and oven-broiling also work.

FAJITAS (BEEF OR CHICKEN)

Makes 4 servings

12 warm Basic Flour Tortillas (page 50), or store-bought, heated (page 34)

2 pounds (910 g) Fajita Beef or Chicken (page 70), keep warm

2 cups (228 g) Grilled or Sauteed Vegetables (page 87), (320 g) thin-sliced white or yellow onion, and (300 g) thin-sliced green and red bell pepper, poblano chiles, or a combination

2 cups (344 g) Refried Pinto Beans (page 83)

2 cups (450 g) Guacamole (page 105)

1 cup (250 g) Pico de Gallo (page 104)

1 cup (230 g) sour cream

Traditionally, fajitas are served with Refried Beans, Guacamole, Pico de Gallo, sour cream, and grilled peppers and onions, all for wrapping inside hot flour tortillas. This is a great dish for homemade tortillas. Make sure they're warm and soft.

1   Preheat the oven to 350°F (180°C, or gas mark 4).

2   Press or shape and bake fresh Basic Flour Tortillas (page 31 and 32) or reheat store-bought tortillas (page 34). Keep warm (page 33).

3   To serve the fajitas, slice the beef or chicken across the grain into strips, about ¼-inch (6 mm) thick and 2 inches (5 cm) long.

4   Arrange a platter with cooked beef and/or chicken, and grilled onions and peppers.

5   Offer with Refried Pinto Beans, Guacamole, Pico de Gallo, and sour cream for assembling the fajitas. Roll the beef or chicken with the desired garnishes in warm flour tortillas.

FAJITA ASSEMBLY TIP

Spread a layer of refried pinto beans on a tortilla. Down the middle of the tortilla, add a few strips of Fajita Beef or Chicken, grilled onions and peppers, Guacamole, Pico de Gallo, and sour cream. Roll like an enchilada or fold like a taco and enjoy. The layer of beans helps hold everything together to prevent spillage.

Taco Salad

Just as California-based Taco Bell led the way in the mass marketing of the crispy taco, we can thank Taco Bell for the introduction of the crispy tortilla salad bowl for taco salad in 1984. Taco Bell mass-marketed it via drive-through windows all over the country. The gimmick spread through fast food outlets and restaurants.

But the origins of the concept are usually traced to Texas. According to Gustavo Arellano, author of *Taco USA: How Mexican Food Conquered America*, Fritos founder Elmer Doolin, based in Dallas, created the dish. His gimmick was a fried bowl made of Fritos dough. In 1955, the dish, then called the Tacup, was on the menu at Disneyland's Casa de Fritos. The taco salad was on its way to fame and fortune.

HOW TO FRY TORTILLA "SALAD BOWLS"

Just as there are multiple gadgets and techniques for frying tortillas for crispy taco shells, there are plenty of molds and ways to fry tortillas for crisp taco salad "bowls." Get one and follow maufacturer's directions or try this technique:

1 Have ready an individual salad or soup bowl of a size the flour or corn tortilla can form a shape around. Place the bowl upside down over a double thickness of paper towels. Or use a tortilla bowl mold.

2 Line a cookie sheet or rimmed baking pan with paper towels.

3 In a deep fryer or electric skillet, heat at least 2 inches (5 cm) of oil to 365ºF (185ºC). Or use a deep skillet or other large pot and a candy/frying thermometer.

4 To fry tortilla "salad bowls," carefully slide 1 tortilla into the hot oil. It should float and bubble. Fry for about 15 seconds. Using tongs, turn and fold over. Fry for another 10 to 20 seconds or until it starts to brown.

5 Use a skimmer or slotted spoon to remove the tortilla from the oil, allowing any exceess to drain back into the pot. Drape the tortilla over the bowl. Allow to drain and cool enough to hold the shape of the bowl. Remove to a lined baking sheet.

6 Repeat with the remaining tortillas.

TACO SALAD

Makes 4 servings

There are so many versions of taco salad that it would be possible to write a whole chapter devoted to recipes for it. We're going to keep it basic, however. This recipe offers two options: making crispy "bowls" of flour tortillas or using crumbled corn tortilla chips as croutons to add crunch to a salad.

1 Prepare Flour Tortilla Salad Bowls or coarsely crumble corn tortilla chips. Set aside.

2 In a large salad bowl, toss together the lettuce, filling(s) of choice, corn if desired, and any other add-ins.

3 Pour the desired salad dressing over the tossed ingredients and toss again to coat evenly.

4 Divide the salad among four Flour Tortilla Salad Bowls or garnish with crushed corn tortilla chips and serve.

Roasted Fresh Corn on the Cob: Preheat the oven to 350ºF (180ºC, or gas mark 4). Remove the husks from 1 or more ears of corn. Lightly brush the corn with vegetable oil. Place on a baking sheet and roast for 30 minutes or until the corn is lightly browned and tender. To remove from the cob, allow to cool 10 minutes and then cut the kernels from the cob. Hold vertically on a cutting board. Using a sharp knife, cut down the length of the cob to shear off the kernels. Repeat until all the kernels are off the cob. An ear of corn yields about 1 cup (164 g).

Cilantro Chile Limette: In a blender jar or work bowl of food processor, combine ⅓ cup (80 ml) of lime juice, ¾ cup (175 ml) of vegetable or cold pressed extra-virgin olive oil, ½ cup (8 g) lightly packed cilantro leaves, 1 clove of garlic, 1 small serrano chile (stem removed and seeded if desired), and 1 teaspoon salt. Process for 2 to 3 minutes or until smooth.

4 large Basic Flour Tortillas (10 inches or 25 cm or larger) (page 50), or store-bought, crisped to make "salad bowls" (page 164 and 167) or 2 cups (480 g) crumbled Fried Tortilla Chips (page 110), or store-bought

8 cups (576 g) torn iceberg or of romaine lettuce, or a combination

2 cups (450 g) or a combination of heated fillings, such as:
• Ground Beef Filling (page 68)
• Shredded Beef Brisket (page 69)
• Fajitas, Beef or Chicken (page 70)
• Shredded Braised Pork (page 71)
• Carnitas (page 71)
• Shredded Spicy Chicken (page 74)
• Roast Duck (page 75)
• Shrimp, Sautéed or Fried (page 76)
• Fish, Sautéed or Fried (page 77 and 78)
• Pinto Beans (page 80)
• Black Beans (page 81)

1 cup (164 g) roasted corn (see below)

Other options, as: ½ cup (50 g) chopped green onions, ½ cup (72 g) chopped roasted green chiles, 1 cup (104 g) sliced pickled jalapeños (drained)

DRESSING FOR WILTED SALAD

1 cup warm Queso (page 99) or Avocado Crema (page 106)

DRESSING FOR CHILLED SALAD

1 cup (240 g) room temperature Avocado Crema (page 106) or Cilantro Chile Limette (see above)

BELIEVE IT OR NOT

There's a Mexican superstition that dropping a tortilla means you will get a lot of unwanted, unexpected company. Where's the five-second rule when you need it?

MEXICAN SEAFOOD COCKTAIL

Makes 4 servings.

Cocktail Sauce:

1 cup tomato clam cocktail, such as Clamato Juice.

1 cup ketchup

2 tablespoons (30 ml) olive oil

1 medium tomato, seeded and finely chopped to make 1 cup

1 small jalapeno, seeded, finely chopped

½ cup chopped red or white onion

½ cup chopped fresh cilantro

2 tablespoons fresh orange juice

2 tablespoons fresh lime juice

1 tablespoon (15 ml) Mexican hot sauce, such as Cholula, Valentina, or Tapatio, or to taste

1 tablespoon (15 ml) Worcestershire sauce (optional), or to taste

Seafood:

2 pounds (900 g) chilled medium cooked shrimp, peeled, or if using additional seafood below, 1-pound (450 g) chilled medium cooked shrimp, peeled

1 pound (450 g) total of any combination of cooked calamari (squid); 8 to 16 small raw oysters, shucked and juices reserved; 8 to 16 small raw clams, shucked and juices reserved; and lump crabmeat (optional)

1 teaspoon salt, or to taste

1 large avocado, peeled and chopped

Fried Tortilla Chips, (page 110) or store bought

Whether served as a main or a starter, no dish speaks *coctel de mariscos* with more fluency than this one. The recipe is a mash up of several variations. One style called Vuelve a la Vida is known as a hangover cure. The name translates to "return to life" and has roots in the state of Veracruz on the Mexican Gulf Coast. Another similar style emanates from Campeche on the Yucatan Peninsula and is called *Campechano de Mariscos*.

This seafood cocktail is delicious whether you make it with shrimp or a combination of shrimp, squid, oysters, clams, and crab. Crisp, well-salted tortilla chips are the accompanying crunch of choice.

Use cooked shrimp if you want to shortcut the process a bit. Or boil your own, including the squid. Of course, if you're using raw seafood, make sure the oysters and clams are exquisitely fresh.

Having the sauce ready and the seafood chilled makes final assembly easy. Serve in chilled goblets or sundae or parfait glasses. Top with chopped avocado. Offer plenty of tortilla chips.

1 In a medium container or a pitcher with a tight-fitting lid, blend the tomato clam cocktail, ketchup, and olive oil until well-mixed. Fold in the tomato, jalapeno, onion, cilantro, and orange and lime juices. Adjust the seasoning to taste with the addition of Mexican hot sauce and optional Worcestershire.

2 Cover tightly and refrigerate at least 1 hour and up to a day ahead.

HOW TO BAKE FLOUR TORTILLA "SALAD BOWLS"

It is simpler to bake flour tortillas to make a crispy bowl for taco salad. Bake them in molds (available in specialty stores and in kitchenware departments). Or try using inverted muffin tins, as below.

1 Preheat the oven to 350ºF (180ºC, or gas mark 4). Heat a comal or griddle.

2 Have ready several small or large muffin pans. You will use them upside down.

3 Place the tortillas, one at a time, on the hot comal or griddle just long enough to soften.

4 Lightly brush both sides of the softened tortilla with vegetable oil.

5 Place the tortilla in the space between 4 muffin cups on an inverted muffin tin. This will form a bowl shape. Repeat until all the tortillas are positioned in bowl shapes on inverted muffin tins.

6 Place into the heated oven and bake for 20 minutes or until crisp.

TO COOK SHRIMP

In a large saucepan over high heat, combine 8 cups of water, 3 bay leaves, and 1 head garlic, cut in half. When water boils, add 1 tablespoon salt. Stir to dissolve, then add shrimp. Cook for 2 to 3 minutes or just until pink. Remove shrimp from cooking liquid using a slotted spoon. Place in a colander to drain. Peel when cool enough to handle. Chill.

TO COOK CALAMARI

Cut squid bodies into ⅛-inch (4 mm) wide rings. Halve the tentacles lengthwise. Add calamari to boiling water used to cook shrimp. Cook about 1 minute or until cooked through and white. Remove calamari from cooking liquid using a slotted spoon. Drain in colander with shrimp. Chill.

3 To assemble the dish, reserve 8 whole shrimp for garnish. Coarsely chop the remaining shrimp into 1-inch (2.5 cm) pieces. In a large bowl, combine the chopped shrimp and other seafood, including juices from oyster and clams, if using. Pour the chilled cocktail sauce over the seafood and mix well. Add salt as needed to taste. Chill for 30 minutes to 1 hour.

4 Just before serving, chop the avocado. Spoon the seafood mixture into chilled goblets or sundae or parfait glasses. Top with chopped avocado and hang 2 reserved whole shrimp on the lips of each dish. Serve with plenty of corn tortilla chips.

SOP IT UP: SOUPS AND STEWS THAT BEG FOR TORTILLAS

When it comes to Mexican- and Southwestern-style soups and stews, tortilla soup and chili (con carne) are probably the best known. But there are so many more. And all are natural partners of fresh, homemade tortillas. What could be nicer on a weekend than to concoct a big pot of steaming flavor and love? Let it simmer and anticipate the flavors as the delicious aroma wafts from the kitchen. When it's time to eat, whip up a dozen or more fresh tortillas to go with. Then take a bow as a culinary maestro.

TORTILLA SOUP

Makes 8 servings

1 tablespoon (15 ml) vegetable oil

1 cup (160 g) chopped white or yellow onion

2 cloves of garlic, crushed

1 can (8 ounces, or 225 g) of tomatoes with green chiles

4 cups (946 ml) Spicy Chicken Broth (page 74), or store-bought

1 can (8 ounces, or 245 g) of tomato sauce

2 teaspoons chili powder

1 teaspoon ground cumin

1 teaspoon salt, or to taste

1 teaspoon ground black pepper, or to taste

4 Corn Tortillas (page 38), or store-bought

Vegetable oil, for frying

1½ cups (360 g) Spicy Chicken (page 74)

Garnishes: Grated Monterey Jack cheese, chopped avocado, sour cream, lime wedges

Since first published in *The Texas Holiday Cookbook* in 1998, my version of this Southwestern classic has become a staple in my home and the homes of friends. The deep red broth filled with tender chicken looks beautiful with chopped avocado on top. Crisp tortilla strips are a crunchy garnish. It will be a favorite in your kitchen as well.

1 In a large saucepan or Dutch oven over medium heat, warm the vegetable oil. Add the onions, and cook for 3 minutes or until soft. Add the garlic and cook for 1 minute longer or until it releases its aroma.

2 Add the tomatoes with green chiles, Spicy Chicken Broth, and tomato sauce.

3 Stir in the chili powder, cumin, salt, and pepper. Bring the liquid to a boil. Reduce the heat and simmer for 30 minutes.

4 While the soup simmers, in a small skillet over medium high heat, warm 1-inch (2.5 cm) of vegetable oil to 350ºF (180ºC). Fry the tortilla strips in batches for about 3 minutes or until crisp. Drain on paper towels.

5 Add the chicken to the soup and heat through.

6 Garnish individual servings with tortilla strips and as desired with cheese, avocado, and sour cream. Serve with a lime wedge.

Q: *Did you know they were making a movie about a burrito?*
It's a wrap.

CHILI CON CARNE

Makes 4 servings

1½ (680 g) pounds coarse ground beef for chili

½ pound (225 g) lean ground beef

3 cloves of fresh garlic, finely chopped

4 tablespoons (30 g) chili powder

1 tablespoon (7 g) ground cumin

1 cup (235 ml) beef stock or as needed

3 cups (825 g) Tex-Mex Chili Gravy (page 90), New Mexico Red Chile Sauce (page 91), or 1 can (28 ounces, or 795 g) of red enchilada sauce, such as Old El Paso or Las Palmas brand

Garnishes: Grated cheddar, finely chopped white onion, sour cream, Pinto Beans (page 80)

This is a bit of a different technique for making chili, that elixir associated with the historic Chili Queens of San Antonio, who sold it from street carts. This version uses Tex-Mex Chili Gravy (page 90) or New Mexico Red Chile Sauce (page 91) to shortcut the process and produce a lovely, smooth sauce for the stew. Combining ground beef with coarse ground beef for chili is your secret weapon. The finer textured ground beef "melts" into the broth giving an even meatier, luxurious texture.

Note that the list of garnishes includes pinto beans. I'm just too Texan to ever put beans in chili, but I concede that you might want to add some as a garnish. Just please don't add kidney beans!

1 Heat a large saucepan or Dutch oven over medium heat. Crumble the beef into the hot pan, and cook until the meat is no longer pink, stirring occasionally. Continue to cook for another 5 minutes or until the pan juices evaporate and the beef is almost dry.

2 Stir in the garlic and cook for about 1 minute to release its aroma.

3 Stir in the chili powder and cumin. Cook for 1 to 2 minutes, mixing well to evenly coat the meat.

4 Add the beef stock and bring to a boil.

5 Lower the heat and stir in the Tex-Mex Chili Gravy, New Mexico Red Chile Sauce, or canned enchilad sauce. Simmer uncovered for 2 hours, or until the meat is tender.

6 Garnish individual servings as desired.

PINTO OR BLACK BEAN SOUP

Makes 10 servings

2 cups (500 g) dry pinto or black beans

4 strips of bacon, cut into 1-inch (2.5 cm) pieces

1 cup (160 g) chopped yellow or white onions

2 cloves of garlic, finely chopped

6 cups (1.4 L) water, Spicy Chicken Broth (page 74), vegtable stock, or store-bought

3 bay leaves

1 fresh epazote sprig (optional)

1 fresh jalapeño, dried chile arbol, or ¼ teaspoon cayenne pepper

1½ teaspoons salt, or to taste

Garnishes: slices of fresh avocado, Pico de Gallo (page 104), chopped cilantro leaves, grated cheddar, Colby Jack, Monterey Jack, or queso fresco

Whether you like your bean soup with a thin stock or thickened with a puree of flavorful pinto or back beans, you will find this version to be a best friend for fresh tortillas. Use corn tortillas for pinto beans and flour tortillas for black beans. Unless, of course, you want to change things up.

1   Pick through the beans to remove any impurities or shriveled beans. Place in a large bowl with enough water to cover. Remove any beans that float. Pour the beans and water into a colander to drain. Rinse the beans thoroughly with cold water.

2   In a large saucepan over medium-high heat, cook the bacon until translucent. Add the onions and cook for 3 minutes or until soft. Add the garlic and cook for 1 minute longer to release its aroma.

3   Add the liquid, the rinsed beans, bay leaves, epazote, and jalapeño or dried chile or cayenne. Over high heat, bring to a boil.

4   When the liquid boils, reduce the heat, cover, and simmer for 2 to 3 hours or until the beans are soft.

5   Ingredients also may be combined and cooked in a slow cooker for 4 to 5 hours or until the beans are soft.

6   When the beans are tender, add salt. Adjust the seasoning to taste. Remove the bay leaves and epazote sprig before serving.

7   For a creamier consistency, use a slotted spoon to remove 2 cups (344 g) of cooked beans to a medium bowl. Add 1 cup (235 ml) of bean liquid. Mash with the back of a spoon or process until smooth using an electric mixer or immersion blender. Stir back into the soup.

8   Garnish individual servings as desired.

RED OR GREEN POSOLE

Makes 8 servings

2 pounds (910 g) pork shoulder

1½ cups (240 g) chopped white or yellow onion

4 cloves of garlic, finely chopped

4 cups (660 g) canned or frozen posole or hominy, white or yellow, rinsed and drained or fresh Posole (page 42)

3 cups (432 g) chopped fresh roasted red or green chiles (page 40) or 2 containers (14 ounces, or 390 g each) of frozen red or green chile, thawed

4 cups (946 ml) Spicy Chicken Broth (page 74), Pork Broth (page 71), or store-bought

3 bay leaves

Garnishes: Dried Mexican oregano; finely chopped white onion; finely chopped fresh cilantro leaves, lime wedges

Use hominy or posole in this delicious soup. You can make Fresh Posole (page 42) or buy frozen fresh pozole. Canned hominy works just fine as well. The background broth can be colored and flavored by red or green chiles. This dish is as often served for a weekend brunch dish as it is for a weekday lunch. Fresh made tortillas make it even better.

1 Trim the fat from the pork shoulder and cut the meat into 1-inch (2.5 cm) pieces.

2 Heat a large saucepan or Dutch oven over medium heat. Add several pieces of trimmed pork fat and allow to melt and render enough fat to coat the bottom of the pan.

3 Add half of the pork. Cook for 5 minutes, stirring occasionally, or until meat is brown on all sides. Using a slotted, spoon, remove the meat from the pan, reserving the meat and juices. Repeat to brown the rest of the meat.

4 Add the onion and cook for 5 minutes or until the onion is soft and the edges are golden. Stir in the garlic and cook for 1 minute longer.

5 Return all the meat and juices to the pan. Add the pozole or hominy, red or green chile, chicken stock, and bay leaves.

6 Over high heat, bring the liquid to a boil. Reduce the heat and simmer for 1 to 2 hours or until the pork is tender.

7 Remove the bay leaves before serving. Garnish individual servings as desired.

SPOON-FED

"One of the cowboys on the ranch used to brag about the superiority of Mexico versus Spain. What was his measure? Spain eats with silver spoons every day. Mexico eats with their spoons only once. Get it? Tortillas are edibles spoons."

—Charlie Schreiner IV (aka "Four"), senior partner and fourth generation to operate the historic Y.O. Ranch in Kerrville, Texas

CALDO DE RES (BEEF VEGETABLE SOUP)

Makes 8 servings

1 pound (455 g) beef shank, sliced 1-inch (2.5 cm) thick

2 pounds (910 g) beef stew meat, cut into 1-inch (2.5 cm) cubes

2 quarts (1.9 L) water or Beef Broth (page 69)

2 tablespoons (36 g) beef base, or 3 to 4 bouillon cubes

1 cup (160 g) coarsely chopped white or yellow onions

3 cloves of garlic, finely chopped

2 teaspoons salt, or to taste

2 teaspoons ground black pepper, or to taste

2 bay leaves

1 pound (455 g) (about 12) small unpeeled new potatoes

1 cup (90 g) coarsely chopped cabbage

1 cup (180 g) tomatoes, cut into 1-inch (2.5 cm) chunks

1 cup (100 g) celery, cut into 1-inch (2.5 cm) pieces

1 cup (130 g) carrots, cut into 1-inch (2.5 cm) pieces

1 cup (120 g) zucchini, calabacitas (Mexican green squash), or yellow squash, cut into 1-inch (2.5 cm) chunks

2 ears of corn, cut into 2-inch (5 cm) lengths

Lime wedges

½ cup (8 g) coarsely chopped cilantro leaves

Red Rice (page 85)

Garnishes: Chopped fresh cilantro leaves, dried leaf Mexican oregano, chopped white onion, lime wedges

Often simply called "caldo," this beef vegetable soup gets its viscosity from beef shank. It is full of big chunks of potato, squash, cabbage, carrots, and corn. Caldo is usually served with a side of Red Rice (page 85) for stirring in as well as a lime wedge for squeezing into the broth to brighten it. In restaurants, it is often served as a late weekend brunch or weekday lunch. Made in your kitchen, it is great any time.

Don't be shy about picking up the pieces of beef shank and corn to eat with your hands. That's the way it's done. Just let it cool enough so you don't get burned.

1 In a large stockpot or Dutch oven over high heat, combine the beef shank, stew meat, water or Beef Broth, beef base, onions, garlic, salt, pepper, and bay leaves. Bring to a boil over high heat and then reduce the heat, cover, and simmer for 2 hours or until the meat is very tender. Occasionally during cooking time, skim any foam or scum that accumulates at the edges of the pot or the surface of the soup.

2 When the meat is tender, add the potatoes, cabbage, tomatoes, celery, and carrots. Simmer for 10 minutes. Add the zucchini or yellow squash and corn. Cook for another 5 minutes, or until the potatoes are tender when pierced with a fork.

3 Set aside off the heat for 15 to 20 minutes before serving. Remove the bay leaves.

4 To serve, ladle the beef and vegetables into large soup bowls with plenty of broth.

5 Serve Red Rice on the side. Garnish individual servings as desired.

CARNE GUISADA (BEEF STEW)

Makes 8 servings

1 tablespoon (13 g) butter plus 1 tablespoon (15 ml) vegetable oil

2 pounds (910 g) beef stew meat, cut into ¾-inch (19 mm) pieces

1 cup (160 g) chopped white onion

1 cup (180 g) chopped tomato

2 cloves of garlic, finely chopped

1 teaspoon ground cumin

4 cups (946 ml) water or Beef Broth (page 69), or store-bought

¼ cup (61 g) tomato sauce

½ teaspoon dried leaf Mexican oregano, marjoram or thyme

2 bay leaves

1 teaspoon salt, or to taste

1 teaspoon black pepper, or to taste

2 tablespoons (28 ml) vegetable oil

2 tablespoons (16 g) all-purpose flour

This simple stew may be eaten many ways: as a thick soup with sides of Red Rice (page 85), and Refried Pinto Beans (page 83) and, of course, fresh tortillas, corn or flour. Carne Guisada also makes a great breakfast entree, topped with a fried egg and a side of Breakfast Potatoes (page 139).

1 Heat a large saucepan or Dutch oven over medium-high heat. Add the butter and vegetable oil. When the butter melts, add the meat and cook for 5 minutes or until lightly browned on all sides.

2 Add the onion and tomato. Cook for 3 minutes or until the onion is soft. Stir in the garlic and cumin. Cook for 1 minute longer.

3 Add the water or Beef Broth and tomato sauce, oregano, bay leaves, salt, and pepper. Bring to a boil and then reduce the heat, cover, and simmer for 1 hour or until the beef is tender.

4 When the meat is tender, heat a small skillet or saucepan over medium heat. Add the oil and then whisk in the flour. Stirring constantly, cook until the flour is the color of café au lait to make a light, creamy brown roux. Set aside off the heat. Add a small amount of liquid from the stew pot and stir to remove any lumps.

5 Stir the flour mixture into the stew, mixing well. Simmer for another 10 minutes or until the stew is thickened. Remove the bay leaves before serving.

PUERCO GUISADA (RED CHILE PORK STEW)

Makes 6 servings

1 boneless pork butt (shoulder) (2 pounds, or 910 g)

1 tablespoon (15 ml) vegetable oil

1 cup (160 g) chopped white or yellow onion

2 cloves of garlic, finely chopped

2 cups (475 ml) water, Spicy Chicken Broth (page 74), or Pork Broth (page 71), or store-bought

2 teaspoons ground cumin

1 teaspoon salt

1 teaspoon black pepper

¾ teaspoon dried leaf Mexican oregano, marjoram, or thyme

3 cups (825 g) New Mexico Red Chile Sauce (page 91); or 1 can (28 ounces, or 785 g) of red enchilada sauce, such as Old El Paso or Las Palmas brand

This is a pork variation on chili con carne. Instead of being cubed, however, the pork is shredded. Try it over Breakfast Potatoes (page 139) with fried or scrambled eggs on the side. Or, like Carne Guisada, as a stew with sides of Refried Beans (page 83) and Red Rice (page 85). Don't forget the tortillas to sop up the juices.

1 Heat a large saucepan or Dutch oven over medium high heat. Add the oil and cook the pork butt for 5 minutes, turning to brown all sides.

2 Stir in the onion and cook for 3 minutes or until soft. Stir in the garlic and cook for 1 minute longer.

3 Add 2 cups (475 ml) of water or stock, cumin, salt, pepper, and oregano. Bring to a boil and then lower the heat, cover, and simmer for about 2 hours or until the pork is very tender.

4 When the meat is soft enough to shred, set the pot aside off the heat, uncovered, and cool for 30 minutes. Reserve the cooking liquid.

5 When the pork is cool enough to handle, use your fingers or two forks to pull the pork into chunks. Trim and discard any excess fat. Then coarsely shred the meat.

6 Return the pork to cooking liquid. Stir in the New Mexico Red Chile Sauce. Simmer, uncovered, for 30 minutes.

CALDO DE MARISCOS (MEXICAN SEAFOOD STEW)

Makes 8 servings

1 pound (455 g) cleaned squid (optional)

6 cups (1.4 L) water, store-bought fish stock, Spicy Chicken Broth (page 74), or store-bought

1 whole small white or yellow onion, peeled (optional)

2 whole cloves of garlic (optional)

2 cups (360 g) chopped roasted tomatoes (page 101) and their juice or 1 can (15 ounces, or 425 g) of diced fire-roasted tomatoes in juice

2 cups (320 g) coarsely chopped white or yellow onion,

2 cloves of garlic, coarsely chopped

3 chiles guajillo or 2 chiles arbol, rinsed, stems and seeds removed

2 tablespoons (28 ml) vegetable or extra-virgin olive oil

1 pound (455 g) red or white potatoes, unpeeled, each cut into 8 pieces, about 1 x 1-inch (2.5 x 2.5 cm)

3 bay leaves

3 sprigs of cilantro

1½ teaspoons salt, or to taste

1 pound (455 g) mussels, scrubbed and debearded if necessary, or 2 pounds (910 g) unshelled clams

1 pound (455 g) white fish, such as grouper, snapper, halibut, catfish, sea bass, or mahi mahi cut into 1-inch (2.5 cm) cubes

1 pound (455 g) shrimp, peeled and deveined

Garnishes: Chopped avocado, chopped white onion, chopped cilantro leaves, lime wedges

Cioppino lovers rejoice and try this Mexican version. There's a rich red broth, redolent with tomatoes and dried chiles that have been cooked down to concentrate the flavors. It is gorgeous with garnishes of chopped avocado and even more flavorful with a scattering of onions and cilantro. Generous squeezes of lime juice are a must.

Mix and match the seafood as you like. Squid is optional. You'll probably want to choose between mussels and clams. Pick your favorite large flake white fish. Add shrimp if you want.

1 If using squid, rinse the body cavity and tentacles well. Cut into 1-inch (2.5 cm) sections and halve the tentacles if they are large.

2 In a large stockpot or Dutch oven over high heat, combine the squid, water or stock, whole onion, and, if using, whole garlic cloves. Bring to a boil. Reduce the heat and simmer, partially covered, for 25 minutes or until the squid is tender.

3 Strain the liquid into a clean container. Reserve the squid. Discard the onion and garlic. Wipe the stockpot or Dutch oven clean for use in step 7.

4 If not using squid, omit steps 1–3 above.

5 In a blender, combine the tomatoes, onion, and chopped garlic.

6 Tear or cut the dried chiles into small pieces and add to the blender. Process for 2 to 3 minutes or until smooth.

7 In large stockpot or Dutch oven over medium-high heat, warm the oil until it shimmers. It should be hot enough that a drop of water sizzles and splatters. Add the tomato puree all at once, stirring constantly. Cook for 5 to 6 minutes or until darkened in color and the consistency of tomato paste.

8 Measure the reserved squid cooking liquid. If less than 6 cups (1.4 L), add enough water to make 6 cups (1.4 L). Or use 6 cups (1.4 L) fish stock, Spicy Chicken Broth (page 74), or store-bought chicken stock.

9 Stir the stock into tomato mixture. Add the potatoes, bay leaves, cilantro, and salt, stirring to dissolve salt. Reduce the heat to low and simmer for 10 minutes or until the potatoes are fork tender.

10 Just before serving, raise the heat to medium-high. Add the mussels or clams and fish. Cook for 3 minutes or until the bivalves have opened.

11 Add the squid, if using, and shrimp. Remove from the heat and let sit with the lid on for 4 minutes to finish cooking. Remove the bay leaves.

12 Serve in bowls with garnishes on the side.

10

THE FLATBREAD CHAMELEON AND TORTILLA DESSERTS

While most of the recipes in this book have been about fresh tortillas with store-bought tortillas being the backup, this chapter is about innovative ways to use the packaged variety and as shortcuts to deliciousness.

The first recipes in this chapter are devoted to mains and snacks. After that come desserts. And, frankly, several of these would be excellent uses for homemade flour tortillas. Full disclosure: There's a ringer in the dessert category. The recipe for Sopapillas, a type of fry bread, starts with fresh dough instead of prepared tortillas. The dessert sauces at the end can go with almost any of the sweet endings.

Tortillas Fakes

Flour tortillas are versatile and good as subs for fresh pasta, pizza dough, and egg roll wrappers. Like chameleons, flour tortillas can change to meet the occasion. Tortillas can shortcut a lot of recipes that call for doughs. They make great faux dough.

FLOUR TORTILLA "NOODLES" ALFREDO

Makes 4 servings

4 store-bought flour tortillas

2 cups (475 ml) heavy cream

1 package (3 ounces, or 85 g) of cream cheese, coarsely chopped, or ⅓ cup (80 g) mascarpone

6 ounces (170 g) grated Parmesan cheese

1 teaspoon garlic powder

Optional stir-ins: 1 cup (130 g) cooked frozen peas, rinsed and drained; 4 strips bacon or slices of pancetta, crisply fried and crumbled

Flour tortillas can mimic fresh pasta. Roll and cut into "noodles:" thin for fettucine, wide for pappardelle.

1 Tightly roll 1 tortilla. Using a sharp knife on a cutting board, cut the rolled tortilla cross-wise into thin strips like fettucine. Repeat with the remaining flour tortillas.

2 In a medium saucepan over medium heat, cook the cream for 3 minutes or just until bubbles break the surface. Lower the heat and simmer for 5 minutes or until the cream is thickened and reduced to about 1½ cups (355 ml).

3 Whisk in the cream cheese or mascarpone, Parmesan cheese, and garlic powder. Stir and cook for 3 minutes or just until the cream cheese is melted and well-blended. If the sauce is too thick, thin with a bit more cream or milk.

4 Stir in the tortilla "noodles," gently mixing to evenly coat and heat through. Cook for about 1 minute. If desired, stir in green peas. Top with crumbled bacon or pancetta. Serve immediately.

Q: *Where do you find the best tacos?*
In the gulp of Mexico.

FLOUR TORTILLA "NOODLES" CON QUESO

Makes 4 servings

4 store-bought flour tortillas

2 cups (500 g) heated Queso (page 99)

Milk, as needed

**Optional stir-ins:
1 cup (225 g) Homemade Chorizo (page 72), crumbled, cooked, and drained;
1 cup (146 g) coarsely chopped avocado; ½ cup (90 g) chopped tomatoes, rinsed and drained**

Think wide noodles and cheese sauce on this one, or Mexican-style mac and cheese.

1 Tightly roll 1 tortilla. Using a sharp knife on a cutting board, cut the rolled tortilla crosswise into wide strips, like pappardelle or egg noodles. Repeat with the remaining flour tortillas.

2 In a medium saucepan over low heat, combine the heated Queso and stir in the tortilla "noodles," gently mixing to evenly coat and heat through. If the sauce is too thick, thin with milk.

3 Cook for about 1 minute. If desired, stir in Homemade Chorizo. Top with avocado and tomatoes. Serve immediately.

MORE SAUCE AND PROTEIN MATCH-UPS FOR "TORTILLA NOODLES":

- Your favorite barbecue sauce with Beef Brisket (page 69)

- Real Deal Mole (page 94) or Easier Mole (page 96) with Spicy Chicken (page 74), Carnitas (page 71), or Braised Pork (page 71)

- Sour Cream Enchilada Sauce (page 97) with Spicy Chicken (page 74) or Shrimp or Crab (page 76)

FLOUR TORTILLA "PIZZA"

Makes 1 pizza
(1 to 2 servings)

Vegetable oil, as needed

1 flour tortilla (6 inches [15 cm] or 10 inches [25 cm]) (you should make sure that flour tortilla covers the bottom of a cast-iron skillet of the same size)

¼ to ⅓ cup (61 to 81 g) tomato sauce, such as pizza sauce or New Mexico Red Chile Sauce (page 91)

1 cup (115 g) shredded cheese, such as mozzarella or Monterey Jack

½ cup (35 g) cooked Italian sausage, pepperoni, (35 g) Sautéed Mushrooms, (113 g) Homemade Chorizo (page 72), (100 g) Ground Beef Filling (page 68), or desired topping

¼ cup (10 g) coarsely chopped fresh basil, cilantro leaves, or (36 g) roasted green chiles

The object of this exercise is to produce a super easy, very crisp, thin crust pizza. It requires some planning ahead. You need a cast-iron skillet the size of a flour tortilla—a 6-inch (15 cm) or 10-inch (25 cm) skillet will usually match up. Assemble your toppings; heat your skillet. Now, add the tortilla and toppings and crisp the crust. Add the toppings and melt the cheese under the broiler.

You can go any direction you like with toppings. Stay traditional Italian with tomato sauce, Italian sausage, or pepperoni and mozzarella, plus some Parmesan. Or think Mexican food flavors with New Mexico Red Chile Sauce, Ground Beef Filling or Homemade Chorizo, and Monterey Jack. The combinations are as varied as your imagination.

1 Position an oven rack as close as possible to the broiler. Preheat the broiler.

2 Warm a cast-iron skillet over high heat until almost smoking and add just enough oil to lightly coat the bottom. Heat just until the oil shimmers. Lower the heat to medium-high and wipe out most of the oil with a generous ball of paper towels to avoid burning your fingers. Do not remove the skillet from the heat.

3 Add the flour tortilla, small bubbles-side down. Cook for 1 to 2 minutes, or until the bottom crisps and turns brown, and top the puffs. Remove the pan from the heat. **Note:** Flour tortillas appear differently on each side. One side has tiny bubbles, like pebble texture leather and the other side appears smoother with larger bubbles that look like ripples on a pond. The bottom side will crisp. The other side will puff like regular pizza dough.

4 Using the back of a spoon, spread a thin layer of sauce over the surface of the tortilla, spreading sauce all the way to the edge.

5 Sprinkle the cheese over the surface of the tortilla, all the way to the edge.

6 Arrange the sausage or other desired meat topping over the cheese.

7 Place under the broiler for about 3 minutes or just until the cheese melts.

8 Sprinkle with fresh basil, cilantro, or roasted green chiles and serve immediately.

FLOUR TORTILLA "FRIED DUMPLINGS"

Makes 4 servings

2 cups (450 g) cooked Ground Beef Filling (page 68), well-drained, or Shredded Beef Brisket (page 64), Shredded Braised Pork (page 71), or Spicy Chicken (page 74)

1 cup (115 g) shredded Pepper Jack cheese

12 store-bought flour tortillas (6 or 7 inches [15 or 18 cm]), heated (page 34) for pliability

Vegetable oil, for frying

1 teaspoon fine sea salt, or to taste

Salsas and sauces for dipping: Red Salsa (page 101), Roasted Tomatillo Sauce (page 93), Green Tomatillo Sauce (page 93), Chipotle Salsa (page 104), Avocado Crema (page 106), Guacamole (page 105)

This recipe should inspire, not hinder, your imagination. As with many recipes in this book, this is more about the technique. What you fill these bundles with is ultimately up to you. Fillings should be chilled or at room temperature.

1 In a medium bowl, combine the filling and shredded cheese. Stir or knead to combine so the mixture will hold a shape like a meatball.

2 Using a melon baller or a tablespoon, scoop a round of meat and cheese mixture. Place in the center of a tortilla on a cutting board.

3 Fold the tortilla in half, and then fold over to form a triangle. Secure the edges with a toothpick. Repeat until all the tortillas are filled, folded, and secured.

4 In a deep fryer or electric skillet, heat at least 3 inches (7.5 cm) of oil to 375ºF (190ºC). Or use a deep skillet or other large pot and a candy/frying thermometer.

5 Using a slotted spoon, carefully slide a dumpling into the hot oil. Fry 2 to 3 at a time for 15 to 20 seconds, until golden on one side. Using tongs or slotted spoon, turn and cook until golden on the other side, about 15 to 20 seconds longer.

6 Using a slotted spoon, remove the dumplings, allowing any excess oil to drain back into the pot. Place on paper towels to absorb excess grease. Repeat until all the dumplings are fried.

7 Sprinkle with sea salt.

8 Serve warm or at room temperature with the desired salsa or sauce for dipping.

Dessert Dumplings: If you have a sweet tooth, this recipe can be easily modified for dessert. Spread each flour tortilla with ¼ cup of Sweet Mascarpone (page 196) almost to the edges. If desired, add 1 to 2 tablespoons Pumpkin, Sweet Potato, or Rum Apple filling (page 194) to the center of the tortilla. Proceed as above with steps 3 through 6. Sprinkle with cinnamon and sugar. Serve warm or at room temperature with Fruit Pico (page 198), Crème Anglaise (page 196), Dulce de Leche, (page 197), or Pineapple Sauce (page 198), if desired.

Tortilla Desserts

Flour tortillas can shortcut many desserts, such as empanadas, or provide an easy base for Cinnamon Sugar Flour Tortillas "Crepes." The sauces that follow are great with any of these desserts. Use as you will.

SOPAPILLAS (SWEET FRY BREAD)

Makes 16 sopapillas

2¼ cups (281 g) all-purpose flour

2 teaspoons baking powder

1 tablespoon (13 g) sugar, plus additional as needed

¼ teaspoon salt

⅓ cup (68 g) shortening

¾ cup (175 ml) very warm (110°F [43°C]) water

Vegetable oil, for frying

1 cup (340 g) honey

This is the ringer recipe in this chapter because it doesn't begin with a prepared flour tortilla. The texture of a sopapilla is more like fry bread than a flour tortilla, but it is definitely in the extended flour tortilla family.

1   In a large mixing bowl, combine the flour, baking powder, sugar, and salt. Blend well using a large spoon. Or in the work bowl of a food processor, combine the flour, baking powder, sugar, and salt by pulsing once or twice.

2   Using a pastry cutter or fork, combine the shortening and flour mixture until well-blended and crumbly. Or add the shortening to the work bowl of a food processor, pulsing several times until mixture is well-blended and crumbly.

3   Add the water and mix or process until the dough forms. Knead about 20 times or until smooth and elastic. Or remove from the work bowl and knead on a lightly floured board about 20 times or until smooth and elastic. Cover and set aside for at least 30 minutes to rest.

4   Pour the oil into a deep fryer or deep electric skillet to depth of at least 2 inches (5 cm). Preheat to 375°F (190°C). You may also use a deep skillet or dutch oven and a candy or frying thermometer on the stovetop. Fill with 2 inches (5 cm) of oil and preheat to 375°F (190°C).

5   Lightly sprinkle flour on the counter or a large wooden board.

6   Divide the dough into four sections.

7   Roll each section of dough to about 8-inch (20 cm) square, about ⅛-inch (3 mm) thick. Sprinkle the surface lightly with flour to prevent sticking.

8   Using a knife, cut the pastry into 4 squares (4 inches, or 10 cm) or use a cookie cutter of about the same size.

9   Fry each sopapilla in hot oil, about 15 to 20 seconds or until golden on one side. Using tongs or a slotted spoon, turn and cook until golden brown, about 15 to 20 seconds longer.

10 Using a slotted spoon, remove the sopapilla and drain on paper towels.

11 Sprinkle the tops of the warm sopapillas generously with sugar.

12 Serve drizzled with honey.

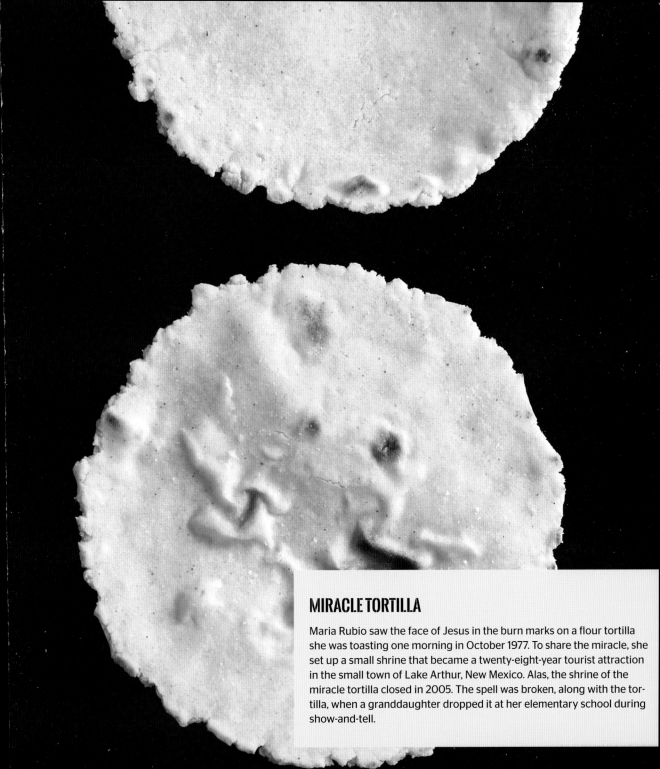

MIRACLE TORTILLA

Maria Rubio saw the face of Jesus in the burn marks on a flour tortilla she was toasting one morning in October 1977. To share the miracle, she set up a small shrine that became a twenty-eight-year tourist attraction in the small town of Lake Arthur, New Mexico. Alas, the shrine of the miracle tortilla closed in 2005. The spell was broken, along with the tortilla, when a granddaughter dropped it at her elementary school during show-and-tell.

FLOUR TORTILLA "CREPES"

Makes 8 crepes

8 tablespoons
(112 g) butter

8 Basic Flour
Tortillas (page 50),
or store-bought

1 cup (230 g) Sweet
Mascarpone
(page 196)

2 cups Crème
Anglaise (page 196),
warm Cajeta
(page 197), Dulce de
Leche (page 197), or
Pineapple Sauce
(page 198)

1 cup (145 g)
rinsed and dried
blueberries or
(125 g) raspberries,
(170 g) sliced
strawberries or
(150 g) bananas

Whipped cream
(optional)

Ground nutmeg
(optional)

The simplicity of this recipe makes it a great one for using fresh homemade flour tortillas. Of course, that sort of defeats the purpose of subbing tortillas for crepes. Just sayin' . . . Use a saute or crepe pan to make these faux crepes.

1   Preheat the oven to 300°F (150°C, or gas mark 2).

2   In a small saute or crepe pan over low heat, melt 1 tablespoon (14 g) of butter. When the butter bubbles, using tongs, add 1 tortilla and swirl to evenly coat one side with butter.

3   Turn and coat second side with butter. The tortilla should be soft; do not allow it to crisp in the butter.

4   Place the tortilla on a large sheet of foil.

5   Repeat with the remaining tortillas, stacking them on top each other. When they all have been softened in butter, wrap the tortillas tightly in foil and place in the oven for 10 minutes.

6   When ready to serve, remove the tortillas from the oven. Spread 2 tablespoons (29 g) of Sweet Mascarpone down the middle of a tortilla. Roll like an enchilada or fold like a taco. Top with the desired fruit. Drizzle with Crème Anglaise or ¼ cup (60 ml) of your desired sauce. Dollop each with whipped cream if desired. Sprinkle with nutmeg.

FLOUR TORTILLA "EMPANADAS"

Makes 8 servings

8 store-bought flour tortillas, heated (page 34)

2 cups (480 g) filling: Pumpkin (page 195), Sweet Potato (page 195), or Rum Apple (page 194)

1 large egg, beaten, plus 1 tablespoon (15 ml) water, milk, or cream

Vegetable oil, for deep frying

1 cup (200 g) sugar

1 tablespoon (7 g) cinnamon

Flour tortillas make a convenient stand-in for empanada dough. You can fill them with various fruit fillings. Prepared pie filling is another useful shortcut.

1   Heat the tortillas for pliability and keep warm. Place 1 tortilla on a cutting board or flat plate. Place ¼ cup (60 g) of filling down on the center of tortilla.

2   Brush the egg mixture around the edge of the tortilla using a ½-inch (12 mm) wide pastry brush.

3   Fold the tortilla edges together. Use your fingers to mash together, crimping the edges. Or, use a fork to press the edges together. For insurance, use a toothpick to secure the edges.

4   In a deep fryer, electric skillet, or heavy skillet over medium-high heat, heat at least 2 inches (5 cm) of vegetable oil to 375ºF (190ºC).

5   Using a metal slotted spoon, carefully slide a tortilla "empanada" into the hot oil. Fry for 45 seconds to 1 minute or until golden brown on one side. Turn and fry on other side for 30 to 45 seconds or until golden brown.

6   Using a spoon, lift the "empanada" out of the hot oil, allowing any excess oil to drain back into the pot. Drain on paper towels. Repeat with remaining empanadas until all are cooked.

7   Combine the sugar and cinnamon. Sprinkle the tops of the warm "empanadas" generously with cinnamon sugar.

8   Serve warm or at room temperature.

CINNAMON SUGAR FLOUR TORTILLA CRISPS

Makes 4 servings

4 Basic Flour Tortillas (6 to 7 inches, or 15 or 18 cm) (page 50), or store-bought

4 tablespoons (55 g) butter, softened or melted

1 cup (200 g) sugar, plus 1 tablespoon (7 g) cinnamon, well-blended

Sweet Mascarpone (page 196)

1 cup (240 g) Fruit Pico, drained (page 198)

This recipe is a sweet take on Arizona Cheese Crisps. Top with Sweetened Mascarpone and Fruit Pico, an adaptation of Pico de Gallo fresh salsa.

1 Preheat the oven to 350°F (180°C, or gas mark 4).

2 Using a rubber spatula or brush, evenly coat one side of each tortilla with butter all the way to the edges. Arrange the buttered tortillas in a single layer on a baking sheet.

3 Place the tortillas in the oven and bake 10 minutes or until lightly toasted and crisp.

4 Remove from the oven and generously sprinkle the surface of each tortilla with the sugar cinnamon mixture.

5 Serve each crisp with a dollop of Sweet Mascarpone or cream cheese.

6 Top with ¼ cup (60 g) of Fruit Pico.

Fillings and Sauces for Tortilla Desserts

These delicious fillings are for empanadas or crepes. They can also be used as dips or toppings for dessert, like in Tortilla Crisps or Sopapillas.

RUM APPLE FILLING

Makes 2 cups (480 g)

4 cups (600 g) coarsely chopped apples, peeled and cored

3 tablespoons (45 ml) water

2 tablespoons (28 g) butter

1 teaspoon cinnamon

⅓ cup (67 g) sugar

⅓ cup (50 g) dark raisins

1 tablespoon (8 g), plus 1 teaspoon cornstarch

2 tablespoons (28 ml) rum or orange juice

1   In a medium saucepan over medium heat, combine the apples, water, butter, cinnamon, and sugar.

2   Stir and cook to dissolve the sugar. When the sugar is dissolved and the mixture bubbles, lower the heat. Stir in the raisins.

3   Cover and simmer, stirring occasionally, for 5 minutes, or until the apples are soft.

4   In a small dish, combine the cornstarch and rum or orange juice. Stir into the apples, and cook for about 1 minute or until the apples bubble and thicken. Set aside off the heat and cool completely before using to fill Flour Tortilla "Empanadas" (page 192). Top with Crème Anglaise (page 196).

Q: *What boy band did a commercial for Taco Bell?*
Juan Direction.

PUMPKIN FILLING

Makes 2 cups (480 g)

1 can (15 ounces, or 425 g) of solid pack pumpkin (not pumpkin pie filling)

2 tablespoons (30 g) brown sugar

1 teaspoon ground cinnamon

1 In a medium bowl, using an electric mixer, blend the pumpkin, brown sugar, and cinnamon until the brown sugar dissolves and the ingredients are well blended.

2 Use to fill Empanadas (page 192). Top with Cajeta (page 197) or Dulce de Leche (page 197).

SWEET POTATO FILLING

Makes 2 cups (480 g)

2 cups (656 g) mashed sweet potatoes, fresh baked or canned

1 tablespoon (15 g) brown sugar

1 teaspoon ground cinnamon

1 In a medium bowl, using an electric mixer, blend the sweet potatoes, brown sugar, and cinnamon until the brown sugar dissolves and the ingredients are well-blended.

2 Use to fill Empanadas (page 192). Top with Pineapple Sauce (page 198).

SWEET MASCARPONE

Makes 1 cup (225 g)

8 ounces (225 g) mascarpone or cream cheese

½ cup (100 g) sugar

1 or 2 tablespoons (15 to 30 g) Greek yogurt

Use this as a filling for crepes or as dessert topping for Cinnamon Sugar Flour Tortilla Crisps (page 193). If you can't find mascarpone or just want to use cream cheese, go ahead. Mascarpone is the Italian version of cream cheese, only better.

1 In a medium bowl, combine the mascarpone or cream cheese and sugar.

2 Use an electric mixer to combine the cheese and sugar. To thin the cream cheese, add Greek yogurt as needed to achieve the desired texture.

3 Beat until fluffy. Refrigerate until ready to serve.

CRÈME ANGLAISE

Makes 2 cups (480 g)

¾ cup (175 ml) whole milk

¾ cup (175 ml) heavy cream

4 egg yolks

4 tablespoons (52 g) sugar

2 teaspoons pure vanilla extract

This is a classic custard sauce. It is creamy, eggy, and vanilla-y. In short, it is divine—especially with Flour Tortilla "Empanadas" (page 192). For really easy Crème Anglaise, allow 1 pint of vanilla ice cream to melt in the refrigerator and use it as a sauce.

1 In a medium saucepan over low heat, combine the milk and cream. Heat for 5 minutes or until the liquid simmers and bubbles just break the surface. Remove from the heat.

2 In a medium bowl, whisk together the egg yolks and sugar for 2 minutes or until the sugar dissolves and the mixture is light yellow.

3 Gradually whisk the hot milk mixture into the yolks, stirring constantly. Return the mixture to the saucepan over low heat.

4 Cook and stir for 5 minutes or until the custard thickens and coats the back of a spoon. Do not boil.

5 Remove from the heat. Stir in the vanilla. Allow to cool slightly.

6 Pour the liquid through a fine strainer into a container with tight lid. Cover and chill. Serve chilled.

CAJETA AND DULCE DE LECHE (MEXICAN CARAMEL SAUCES)

Makes 1½ cups (360 g)

4 cups (946 ml) whole goat's or cow's milk

1¼ cups (250 g) sugar

½ teaspoon baking soda

1 teaspoon pure vanilla extract (certified Mexican vanilla if available)

Made with goat's milk, Mexican caramel is a tangy sweet sauce called *cajeta*. If made with cow's milk, the sauce is known as *dulce de leche*. There are shortcut versions. If made in the oven with sweetened condensed milk, I call it EASY Dulce de Leche. Using a crockpot, it is Muy EASY Takes a Long Time Dulce de Leche.

However you make it, this caramel sauce is great for any dessert that begins with tortillas—especially if the dessert includes ice cream. It may also be used like Nutella—as a sweet spread.

1 In a medium-size heavy saucepan over medium heat, combine the milk, sugar, and baking soda.

2 Cook, stirring occasionally with a heat-resistant spatula or wooden spoon, until the sugar dissolves and the milk turns foamy and light, about 15 minutes.

3 Continue cooking at a gentle simmer, frequently stirring and scraping the sides of the pot. Cook for about 45 minutes to 1 hour or until the mixture thickens and turns golden.

4 Stirring constantly, continue cooking until the mixture is thick. It should be sticky enough so that when a spatula scrapes the bottom of the pot, a "trail" remains open for 1 second. Remove from the heat. Stir in the vanilla.

5 Transfer to a heat-resistant widemouthed jar. This may be refrigerated up to 3 months. Reheat gently by placing the jar in saucepan of hot, not boiling, water.

EASY DULCE DE LECHE: WARNING!

Do not try the old-fashioned way by putting a can of sweetened condensed milk in the oven. It's not safe for you or your oven. Instead, place a rack in the middle of the oven and preheat the oven to 425ºF (220ºC, or gas mark 7). Pour the contents of 1 can (14 ounces, or 390 g) of sweetened condensed milk into a 9-inch (23 cm) pie plate. Cover tightly with foil. Set the filled pie plate in a roasting pan. Pour enough very hot water into the roasting pan to come halfway up the side of the pie plate. This is called a water bath. Carefully place the roasting pan water bath on a rack in the hot oven and bake for 45 minutes. Check the water level, adding more if the water has evaporated. Bake for 45 minutes longer or until the milk is thick and brown, i.e., caramelized. Remove the roasting pan from the oven and then remove the pie plate from the water bath. Cool, uncovered. Transfer to a heat-resistant widemouthed jar. It may be refrigerated up to 3 months. Reheat gently by placing the jar in a saucepan of hot, not boiling, water. Makes 1¼ cups (300 g).

Muy EASY Takes a Long Time Dulce de Leche: Remove the paper label from 1 can (14 ounces, or 390 g) of sweetened condensed milk. Place the unopened can in a slow cooker. Add enough water to completely cover the can. Place the lid on the cooker and turn on the "low" setting. Cook for 8 hours. Carefully remove the can from the hot water using tongs and heatproof gloves to a heatproof saucer. Place in the refrigerator for 2 hours. Open the can and scoop the contents into a heat-resistant widemouthed jar. It may be refrigerated up to 3 months. Reheat gently by placing the jar in a saucepan of hot, not boiling, water. Makes 1¼ cups (300 g).

PINEAPPLE SAUCE

Makes 2 cups (280 g)

2 cups (330 g) coarsely chopped fresh pineapple or 1 can (20 ounces, or 560 g) of crushed pineapple

3 tablespoons (42 g) butter

2 tablespoons (26 g) turbinado or granulated sugar

½ teaspoon pure vanilla extract

Pinch of salt

This sauce is great on Flour Tortilla "Crepes" (page 190) or Flour Tortilla "Empanadas" (page 192).

1 In a medium saucepan over medium heat, combine the pineapple, butter, and sugar.

2 Stir and cook to dissolve the sugar. When the sugar is dissolved and the mixture bubbles, lower the heat. Simmer, stirring occasionally, for 5 minutes or until the sauce is thickened and syrupy.

3 Stir in the vanilla and salt.

4 Serve warm or at room temperature.

FRUIT PICO

Makes 4 cups (560 g)

1 pint (340 g) strawberries, hulled and coarsely chopped, to make 2 cups

1 peach or mango, peeled and chopped, to make 1 cup (175 g)

1 Granny Smith apple, unpeeled and chopped, to make 1 cup (125 g)

1 teaspoon lemon juice

Serve this with Cinnamon Sugar Flour Tortilla Crisps (page 193).

1 In a medium bowl, combine the chopped strawberries, peach or mango, and apple.

2 Toss to combine. Stir in the lemon juice.

3 Chill until ready to serve.

Acknowledgements

Thank you to my editor, Dan Rosenberg, and my agent, Dedie Leahy, for making this book happen. Thanks, too, to the rest of the team at The Harvard Common Press, including art director Anne Re, graphic designer Laura McFadden, photographer Kristin Teig, project manager Renae Haines, publicist Lydia Finn, and my hometown recipe testers, Paula Cain and Martha Hershey.

About the Author

Dotty Griffith has tortillas down flat. The Texas author reveres the daily bread of the American Southwest and Mexico. With 30 years of food writing experience and 11 cookbooks, Dotty is an authority on the people's cuisines of her state and region: Tex-Mex, barbecue and chili. Her other titles include *The Enchilada Queen Cookbook* with Sylvia Casares, *The Texas Holiday Cookbook, The Contemporary Cowboy Cookbook, Celebrating Barbecue,* and *Wild About Chili.* She's judged barbecue and chili contest all over Texas and the United States. Her work has appeared in *The New York Times, Money Magazine, The Ladies Home Journal, The Smithsonian Magazine, Travel & Leisure, The Wine Spectator, Modern Luxury: Dallas, Restaurant Business News, Southwest Spirit, Gourmet,* and *The Texas Almanac.* She lives in Dallas and teaches culinary journalism at the University of North Texas.

INDEX